DRESSO

CU00693732

Nandita Pandey is the founder an~~~~ ~~~~ ~~~~~~~~~ strategist of Prismatic Consulting, Chennai. She works in the areas of personal branding, performance coaching and corporate training for clients like CXOs, entrepreneurs and multinationals. She has worked in organizations like NIIT Ltd, GE Capital, RRD Donnelley and Daimler India Commercial Vehicles before starting out as an entrepreneur. She holds the Women Glory Award for her work in the field of personal branding.

DRESSOLOGY
THE SCIENCE OF POWER DRESSING

NANDITA PANDEY

PAN

First published 2018 by Pan
an imprint of Pan Macmillan Publishing India Private Limited
707, Kailash Building
26, K. G. Marg, New Delhi – 110 001
www.panmacmillan.co.in

Pan Macmillan, 20 New Wharf Road, London N1 9RR
Basingstoke and Oxford
Associated companies throughout the world
www.panmacmillan.com

ISBN 978-93-86215-29-1

Typeset by Manmohan Kumar
Printed and bound in India by
Replika Press Pvt. Ltd.

To my parents – the people who influenced
my life the most.

CONTENTS

FOREWORD

THE TERM FASHION LACKS the precision of the word dress for it refers to many different kinds of material and non-material cultural products, for example, houses, music, automobiles, scientific theories, philosophy, recreation. Further, like ornament, it forces positive and negative value judgements on body modifications and supplements their properties on the basis of their relative positions within a fashion cycle of introduction, mass acceptance, and obsolescence. In addition, not all types of dress qualify as fashion. For example, religious dress in many societies resists fashion change and is, therefore, automatically excluded from a study of fashion. Immediate surroundings of space and people can influence interpretations of dress.

Fashion and costume do have some things in common – both express identity. Haute couture is a living art, the purpose of which may be decorative, provocative, humorous, revolutionary, promotional and political. It is an artistic engine that generates income. A fashion designer's goal is to tell stories through her evolving seasonal collections, and to make people look beautiful.

The author of *Dressology*, Nandita Pandey, has sixteen years of rich and diverse experience in learning methodologies and geographies. In this book, she has covered issues which range from image matters to body covering, skin care, power dressing and style icons of India, all of which will be very useful to young entrepreneurs and corporate professionals. The outcome of the book is very commendable and has expectations for more volumes to come.

Prof. Dr Anitha Manohar

Director

National Institute of Fashion Design

PREFACE

MY MOTIVE FOR WRITING this book is not limited to one reason. Although the most compelling reason was to write a book that caters to the Indian population. If you have noticed, most books on image management, power dressing, self-image and presentation are written by non-Indians. These books may be very good but, often, they lack localization. Some of the techniques or steps suggested in these books may not be relevant to us. My experience with corporates, across India, has led me to believe that a book that talks directly to the working Indian man and woman will have a greater impact.

Another reason, which is more of a personal observation, is that Indians are often perceived differently on global platforms. Those who are being exposed to colleagues or customers belonging to other nationalities for the first time are often unsure of how to dress, behave, eat or speak. The resulting first impression that they create is not too great and, in some instances, has led efficient employees to lose good opportunities.

This book will reveal a few easy steps and secrets to help you present yourself appropriately, confidently and successfully in a corporate setting. It is not intended as a step-by-step guide that readers must follow to the T; however, you are encouraged to read it as a story and take away any learning that appeals to you.

INTRODUCTION

YOU ARE GETTING READY for a day at work. You go through your routine and are almost ready to leave. What are you most likely to do before you step out? You take a last look at yourself in the mirror to check if you look good and to see if you have achieved the intended look. If you have an important meeting planned for the day or if you are to meet a new client, you will probably spend a few more minutes in front of the mirror practising a smile, a handshake or a self-introduction. For many of us, this may not be the first time that we are attending a meeting or giving a presentation. Yet, each time there is an innate need to look your best and to be your best. This is because we all know that the people around us look at us, create impressions about us and accordingly judge our capabilities. But what would happen if the control panel were to be in your hands?

Then, people will perceive you the way you want to be perceived.

Yes, this is possible! You can determine what people think of you and how they see you. But it comes with a good deal of practice and a general know-how of corporate etiquette and dressing to create the right impression.

Let's start by determining your Image Quotient. Fill in the questionnaire below and see how you fare. Your image score will divulge the best points about you, areas that require improvement and a general understanding of how you and others perceive you. Let's get started!

WHAT IS YOUR IMAGE QUOTIENT?

Tick one box for each of the fifteen questions that you find most appropriate for yourself. Then, calculate your score based on the number assigned for each of the four options (provided in the score tables below). For example, if I tick 'often' for question 5, the score that I will assign myself will be 4.

	Often	Sometimes	Rarely	Never
1 I am confident about the way I dress up				
2 People identify my job/ personal role when they look at me				
3 I make excuses about the way I am dressed				

	Often	Sometimes	Rarely	Never
4 I feel intimidated by my boss				
5 I get enough opportunities based on my interaction with people				
6 I am confident about talking to people when I walk into a room of strangers				
7 I get positive compliments about my appearance				
8 I am confident about selecting clothes for different occasions				
9 I often have a difference of opinion with my colleagues				
10 My management thinks I need to assert more/less				
11 Other people get more opportunity than me at my workplace				
12 Other people get more visibility and overseas projects than I do				
13 My team members do not listen to me				

	Often	Sometimes	Rarely	Never
14 I experience emotional ups and downs				
15 I find it difficult to maintain rapport with internal/external clients				
Final score				

Scoring for questions 1, 2, 5, 6, 7, 8

Often	4
Sometimes	3
Rarely	2
Never	1

Scoring for questions 3, 4, 9, 10, 11, 12, 13, 14, 15

Often	1
Sometimes	2
Rarely	3
Never	4

To know the analysis of this questionnaire, please enter your score in this URL: www.nanditapandey.com/dressology

'You never get a second chance to make a first impression.'

Andrew Grant

ONE

IMAGE

MANY A TIME WE hear people say don't judge a book by its cover. However, human nature forces us to do just that. We see a book's cover and create an impression about it even before reading the first page. A great cover may entice the reader to immediately buy the book although the book's content itself may not be so great. On the other hand, a reader may walk past a book that has a poor cover even though the story might be incredible.

So what is it that a good book is missing out on? It is missing the attention of its intended readers. It is unable to capture the reader's eye. Now, connect this to how people perceive one another. Just as you see an appealing book, you see a well-dressed, well-mannered individual and you are instantly awestruck by them. Presenting yourself splendidly becomes important, because people do judge one another at the first look.

FIRST IMPRESSIONS AT WORK

How long do you think it takes for a person to create an impression of you? A minute? Five minutes? It takes somewhere between three and thirty seconds. That means in less than half a minute

3 - 30 seconds

Cause and Effect

someone has already judged you. You may think that's way too quick to judge someone but, in fact, there is a rationale behind this number. First impressions have a cause and effect relationship. In less than a minute, there isn't enough time for someone

To speak to you and learn about your personality. People, most likely, see you as a package and your attractiveness as a package determines their impression of you.

So, what can anyone see in a few seconds? How is someone creating their first impression of you? Consciously or unconsciously, people observe the 'Elements of Image' while creating first impressions. Primarily, there are three elements of image:

- Clothes, Grooming and Body language (accessories and etiquette).

CLOTHES   GROOMING   BODY LANGUAGE
accessories and etiquette

None of these require communication. These elements allow another person to create an impression of you at a glance. Imagine the power and vitality of these simple elements. Before we delve deeper into impressions and the elements of image, let's understand how we see ourselves, or rather our own self-image.

SELF-IMAGE

It may sound astounding, but self-image is formed when you are as young as two. Your self-image represents your mental perception of yourself. This image is fairly adamant, and resists change of any kind as it is developed over several years of self-evaluation based on your own experiences, opinions of you and the judgements of others. For example, if you were stout as a kid and your family and friends nicknamed you 'chubby' or 'motu' or any other name based on your physical appearance; you are most likely to have grown up thinking you are still stout even if you have lost weight over the years. No matter how many pounds you might have shed since childhood, your self-image continues viewing you as a chubby person.

Do you know that self-image has a direct relationship with your self-esteem? Having a poor self-image means you are likely to have low self-esteem as well. A subjective investigation of a person reveals their internal qualities and personality. Similarly, an objective investigation reveals physical attributes and other achievements. Therefore, self-image and self-esteem are overlapping concepts.

Now, let's talk about how your image affects you. We all know that looking good equals to feeling good. When you dress smart, you automatically develop poise, maintain a good posture and look more confident. On the other hand, when you know you are dressed poorly, you look awkward and feel uncomfortable. So when one is looking good, they feel good.

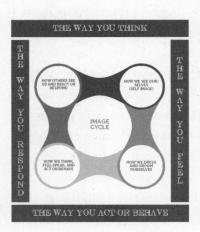

When you feel positive and good, you behave in a positive way and the others also respond in a positive way. This cycle is also true when we do not feel good. The reverse is applicable. These are called 'The Universal Effects of Image'. The way you look has a direct effect on:

- The way you think,
- The way you feel, and
- The way you behave.
- This directly affects how others react or respond to you.

You must know that the universal effects of image functions in a cyclical motion. Others respond based on how you think, feel and behave. In turn, this affects how you see yourself. This cycle continues from day-to-day with you controlling it. So, how do you change it? How do you go about creating a positive universal effect of your image? Think about what you would like to communicate as a first impression. You could choose to be authoritative, capable, approachable, relaxed, or just formal. Once you start seeing yourself the way you choose, others will start seeing you as you see yourself.

THE 5CS OF IMAGE MANAGEMENT

The 5Cs of image management are qualities that you should aim to possess in order to have a great self-image. They are:

1. Congruent – The way you present yourself is arguably the most

important quality in image management. Just because you have a great physique, you cannot be termed an athlete. Similarly, imitating the dressing sense of another person would not guarantee that others would perceive you so! Presentation is unique to you and it is recommended that you never try to fit into the shoes of others. Just dress in a way that suits you and your style!

2. Credible – As the word indicates, credibility is all about being believable and it should reflect in the way you dress. Being credible is an integral value in personal branding and it has to be practiced with consistency and commitment. You can create positive impressions based on your appearance, conduct, verbal communication and body language. Dress in a way that is true to who you are and your values.

3. Charming – Everyone, without exception, would like to appear charming. However, adding charm to your appearance does not simply mean that you wear good-looking attire. Apart from being well-dressed, you need to carry yourself well. You should listen to people, greet people, communicate with them in a way that makes them feel that you are genuinely interested in them. It is important to remember that good looks is in our genes, but looking good is in our hands.

4. Cost effective – Buying and wearing a designer label is not possible every time. It is a proven practice to mix and match garments, fabrics, patterns and colours to create the desired impact rather than buying tons of clothes that

you are not going to wear more than once. Clothes are our primary resources and we should learn to make the most of what we have.

5. Comfortable – Above all, dress so you feel comfortable. Wear styles, colours and fabrics that you are comfortable in. If something does not match your style, culture or value systems, you should not wear that. Always wear clothes in which you feel comfortable and confident. Dress according to your mood and for the occasion. If you are uncomfortable in your clothes, your body language and behaviour automatically changes to reflect an unsure personality. Moreover, you don't want to be in a position where you are constantly fidgeting with or adjusting your clothes. This is not only disturbing to you but distracting to those around you.

Don't we all like it when we get a compliment? We subconsciously pick up clothes to wear in which we have received compliments from others. How many of us have clothes that are never worn in our wardrobe? The reason is we do not think that we look good in them.

Once you are familiar with and can apply the 5Cs of image management to your life, you can go on to managing your image and making it better.

HOW TO MANAGE YOUR IMAGE?

One of the ways to manage your image is personal branding. Personal branding is the art of building a unique brand around you as an individual. It is becoming increasingly important because modern audiences trust the individuals behind the company. The credibility or branding of the person behind the company becomes important in building the organization, getting clients and investors. This is particularly true for start-ups and small- and medium-sized organizations and for professionals. Your personal brand hence is all about being YOU. It talks about your values and what you stand for.

THE NEED FOR PERSONAL BRANDING

People want to do business with other people, not with companies. Putting a strong personal brand on the frontline of your sales process can dramatically improve conversion rates up to 80 per cent. It helps you get more customers because they can see the value that you bring to the table and what you can deliver. They give you a chance to present your products and services. The world can see your values by the brand that precedes your entry into any organization. Personal branding is becoming increasingly essential for the following reasons:

1. Personal branding allows you to be yourself rather than being directed by others as they see fit. You can define your own values.
2. Self-confidence increases as you build a brand. With more value being offered, you enjoy the exercise with much more interest.
3. By doing what you say you are going to do, the credibility factor of your brand increases.

4. You always have a niche that you specialize in. The specialty of your brand increases due to your uniqueness and quality.

5. Creating a personal brand could live forever. Leaving a mark is something that each of us would like to achieve for ourselves.

6. Your brand will stand out from the competition. Being different in the way you offer your service will give you an edge over others.

7. By investing your energy on your own creation, you get the benefit of staying focused and growing your brand considerably faster.

Think about why famous brands tend to use big names in those industries related to their product for advertising. This may make us wonder as to why such superstars are used for advertising a product if the buying decision is based on the quality of the product. It is purely because of the brand value of that individual rather than the product itself. This is the power of personal branding, and everyone has a right to have their own.

Personal branding overview

Creating and developing a brand value for yourself is a process and you need to drive it every day, every moment. The most important aspect in personal branding is creating an identity for yourself. Before creating an identity, you need to know yourself better. The following shows the key steps associated with branding. The 5D framework should make it easy for you to follow.

1. Discover
   - Yourself, your core values/principles
2. Define
   - Your audience, value proposition, purpose
3. Design
   - Your brand, products, strategy to make it visible
4. Deliver
   - On your commitments with consistency
5. Drive
   - Loyalty, relationships, new opportunities

In this process, you can introspect and obtain much clarity when developing your brand. Ask yourself the following questions:

- What is my passion/uniqueness and how could it help others?
- What makes people approach me?
- What is the significant accomplishment in my career that would help someone?
- How do I distinguish myself from the rest of my competition?
- How can I help someone?
- Why does a person come to me rather than someone else?

Following are the three pillars of personal branding

a. Who you are – your education, skills, accomplishments and career history.
b. Who you want to be – your passion, personal goals and career aspirations.
c. How the world perceives what you present – your communication style, behaviour, personality, others'

impression of you and how they would describe you to a friend or co-worker.

The below diagram should give you a fair idea of how you can go about managing your brand. Start with the basics by asking yourself what your personal and professional goals are and then work on a strategy to achieve them.

DISCOVER
Yourself, your core values/ principles

DEFINE
Your audience, value proposition, purpose

DESIGN
Your brand, products, strategy to make it visible

DELIVER
On your commitments with consistency

DRIVE
Loyalty, relationships, new opportunities

Next, list your short-term goals and your long-term goals. You will need to assess two important things first, which will help you achieve your desired goals:

1. Your projection of visual image, and
2. Perception.

Projection of visual image is what you want to display visually to others or what they will see when they meet you. Here is where the three tools of image management come into play:

- Attire
- Etiquette
- Body language

Your projection of these three tools decides how others see you. Using these tools to better your image will help you recreate your impression on people. In this book, we will focus on attire or dressing.

Perception ideally means how you or someone understands something. There are three facets to perception when it comes to image management.

1. Who am I?
2. How I perceive myself.
3. How others perceive me.

There must be a correlation between these three points for your image to be consistent, powerful and lasting.

Academically, image management is evaluating and controlling the impact of your appearance on yourself and others, which also impacts the achievement of your goals. Therefore, the appearance that you create must boost your professional image. However, let's not mistake appearance, in this case, to mean only your looks. It also includes your behaviour, the value you give to yourself and your respect for others. It also encompasses your outlook towards social situations, occasions, your various roles and ambitions. For each role that you play, you may want a different image to be projected. However, the basic values that you have will remain the same. You can tweak the image that you wish to create using image management.

Start by managing your image at home and in your community. Try modifying your roles at home, your behaviour at occasions and develop a favourable image of yourself in the community. Achieving this is sure to give you some confidence. Then, start the same at your workplace. An important aspect of personal image management is your sense of self. Our professional presence says a lot about our capabilities and attitude. This can attract others and interest them in what you have to say. As your sense of self changes, you will see a visible difference in how people perceive you.

Most of us think we know it, but a deeper look will make us realize that there is much more to image. Remember, knowing is not doing; doing is doing. What we may know are the basics, but not the how and why, hence, we do it inconsistently.

Bad News – People have formed impressions about you and they are treating you based on these impressions. If you feel that people don't treat you the way you want them to or the way they should, then it is time for you to work on your image.

Good News – You still can change your image (it will take a little more effort). Rework is always extra effort than the first time done right. Managing your image can be learned and practiced until it becomes a natural part of your personality.

IMAGE CONSULTING

It would be apt to say that image consulting is an art. It helps individuals manage their appearance and pair it up with soft skills to portray a confident personality. It helps create powerful impressions that open doors to more and better opportunities where one can use one's skills to make the best of those opportunities. Therefore, as an artist, the image consultant is always on her toes to create empowering personalities. Each client is different with different needs and goals. Image consulting involves continuously learning about a client and providing feedback and guidance to the client, which then translates into visible transformation. The ultimate aim is to achieve a more self-assured and optimistic image. So, even if you are in a group, the image consultant, at some point, must analyze each one as a separate individual.

Often, image consulting seminars involve individual counselling or coaching sessions after the actual workshop. The workshop itself could deal with a range of topics from clothing to make-up to business etiquette and speech. An image consultant could play a variety of roles based on her educational qualifications and expertise. Each client helps enrich the consultant's knowledge base. Therefore, you will notice that all workshops are not exactly the same. More experienced consultants develop their own methods and practices based on their learning and experience. Image consulting is also about keeping up-to-date and understanding current business trends. It is a lifelong learning process for the consultant and, in turn, for the client.

Talking about the field itself, businessmen and professionals are increasingly seeking help from image consultants. Apart from direct benefits of enhancing your image, there are long-term benefits as well. Even those with a great image and self-esteem often find that there are areas that could require constant improvement. Image consulting helps fill those gaps.

THE IMAGE CONSULTANT

An image consultant is someone who looks at you in entirety and manages different aspects of your internal and external self in order to provide you with a better, more enhanced image. He or she knows the nitty gritties of clothes, colours, shapes, textures, accessories, etc. It is also evident from their choice of career that an image consultant loves to socialize and work with people. Their job involves networking, building relationships and making people happier through tailored services. A devoted consultant is usually knowledgeable in an array of complementary skills that facilitate in image building.

As an image consultant, my approach is to look at a client's internal image or what I call 'internal wiring' before looking at the external simply because that is easier. An inside-out approach helps align the behaviour and mindset before addressing the appearance. It is imperative that both be addressed because individuals are seen as a complete package. Nothing about your image or persona should look out of place. If you have achieved uniformity or completeness, it means you have done it right.

People speak with their appearance; you should listen with your eyes.

Did you know that approximately 83 per cent of any communication is said to be visual? For example, when someone walks into a room, you scan that person from head to toe and judge her personality even before she has spoken.

So, how do you speak with your appearance? The idea is simply to create a focal point. Draw attention to what matters and make sure that every other aspect of your personality helps you do that. In most cases, you would like the attention to be drawn to your face and what you say. So, make sure that your clothes, accessories, make-up, etc. complement your face. Carry yourself well and speak confidently. This helps you deliver your message clearly and avoid diversions.

A good tip to remember is that your image must synchronize with your mission or vision. Appear to represent more than your person to achieve your goals.

'In any face to face communication, 55 per cent of the message is delivered through facial expressions. Therefore, it is imperative that people look at our faces while communicating.'
Albert Mehrabien

POINTS TO NOTE

✓ It takes between three and thirty seconds for another person to create an impression of you. These impressions are lasting and people judge you based on these.

✓ The three elements of image are clothing, grooming and body language.

✓ Self-image is created when you are as young as two years old.

✓ Self-image has a direct correlation to self-esteem.

✓ The 5Cs of image management are credible, charming, competitive, correct and comfortable.

TWO

ORIGINS OF POWER DRESSING

THE WORD 'POWER' IN power dressing implies that an individual dresses to highlight their position of importance. Did you know that power dressing is a term that was originally coined for women? In the early 1900s, the corporate structure was primarily occupied by men. Therefore, when women started stepping in, their initial attempt to fit in saw them dressing just like men in straight pants and loose blazers.

In the 1920s, a new era in fashion began with the Coco Chanel suit. Well-fitted collarless jackets with straight knee-length skirts became revolutionary at the

time; a rare statement that women didn't have to camouflage behind men's clothing anymore. In almost a century since its inception, the style has been modified but its elegance and simplicity are still the same. It is not surprising that Coco Chanel still remains the most admired fashion icon the world over.

Suits gave women an air of authority in a male-dominated workforce. Their equality and success depended on being accepted and valued, which at the time, was a monumental task. Once that was achieved, their suits continued to be redesigned too. Through the twentieth century, suits became the definition of power dressing and each decade saw a new influence on women's suits. Eventually, women no longer dressed to ape men but began creating individuality. It was only by the 1980s that power dressing for women became a reality.

This, of course, does not discount the evolution of dressing for men. With regard to formal wear, men's fashion can be traced back to the late 1800s. From Victorian times to the present day, you will notice that men's wear has been ever changing.

Let's go back in time and take a look at the evolution of power dressing for men.

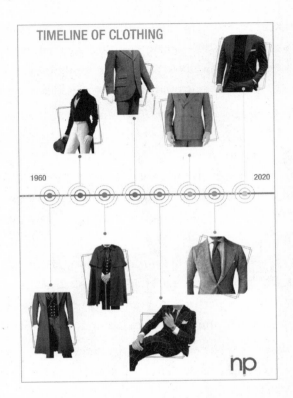

BENEFITS OF DRESSING WELL

'Dress shabbily and they remember the dress; dress impeccably
and they remember the woman' Coco Chanel

Whether you should dress well or not is not the question. It
is essential that you dress well if you want to be successful.
Why does it matter how you present yourself? Because it
directly represents you and your position at work. Always look
professional. Do not just dress yourself; think about whom and

what you are dressing for. You must dress for the audience, the setting, the culture, the company and yourself. You may wonder how dressing well or power dressing is going to help you get anywhere. You will be surprised that it does in a number of ways.

It's a self-confidence booster. The minute you find yourself looking good, you find yourself acting self-assured. For example, you are a working woman. You try getting into a formal navy blue skirt, a white classic shirt, pair it with a sleek navy blue blazer and top it with covered heels. You will find more reason to stare at yourself in the mirror. Your poise and presence are sure to surprise you.

It conveys your attention to detail. Everything should be taken care of, which brings me back to the complete package. From your hair, to your perfume, to your accessories, bags, etc. This shows others how important self-presentation is to you.

You will learn to appreciate the finer things. A well-dressed person eventually understands that simplicity is elegance. When you invest more time in the smaller and finer elements of dressing, it is noticed by others who have a taste for the finer things. Small details as such add up to see you entering a club of refined individuals who dress well.

Your appearance calls for respect. When you look the part, you will feel the part and others will see you the same way. It is just like an actor playing his or her part in a play. If you are acting as a king, you must make sure to dress like one, walk like one and talk like one. Otherwise, you will be seen as just another courtier.

Others will feel respected by you. Imagine dressing well and going to meet a colleague even if it was a casual meeting. He or she will be pleasantly surprised to find you looking dapper. It shows that you care and have great regard for the person you are meeting.

Your first impressions are set. A sudden meeting at work, an after work party or a surprise visit from potential clients; you are prepared to create the best impressions because you are ready. Therefore, it is imperative that you dress well to work every day to manage unforeseen events.

It is great fun. There are many who casually indulge in fashion, shopping and clothes, and it really does not require much effort. Dressing can be fun, if you make it so.

How about drawing some inspiration from popular personalities around the world? People like Ratan Tata, Marissa Mayer, Indra Nooyi and Anand Mahindra are flawlessly dressed every time. They know what to wear, where to wear and how to wear. They influence the global working population today.

COMMON MISTAKES THAT PEOPLE MAKE

It is true that it is easy to go wrong when it comes to dressing for work. Many a time, people holding important positions make blunders that tarnish their image. These may seem like small and simple details, but these details are what make all the difference. The attention you pay to your dress speaks volumes about your attention to detail elsewhere. The way you do one thing, is usually the way you do everything. So, the best practice is to keep up and focus on the particulars.

Think about it for a minute. What are the common mistakes that men make with their office attire? Check if you identify with any of the below scenarios.

1. You are ready for a day at work. You are wearing a light-blue checked shirt; a check-design blue blazer and a blue tie with a pattern. You may think that multiple patterns show sophistication and creativity. However, the complex look might be an overdose.

2. Which one would you pick? A blazer that falls off your shoulders giving you a square shape or one that you have to unbutton before you take a deep breath? Did you go for option one? Well, both are not quite correct. It should be neither too tight nor too loose. Blazers must always be tailor-made to fit you giving your shoulders a firm look.

3. When it comes to suits, do you opt for blues and blacks? Wearing the same clothing or same colour every time is not necessary unless you have a uniform. Go for browns and greys too. Finding ways to mix it up is good for your image.

4. Big digital watches on your hand or a bling buckle on your belt that is engraved might look good at informal settings

and even cause envy among friends. At the workplace, they become objects of distraction that also meddle with your image. As a rule, always match your belt to your shoes.

5. How often have you run to work without giving your shirt a good ironing? It may seem an arduous and unnecessary task, but it creates a very important impression. Wrinkled clothes are a complete no. It shows lack of care and an informal attitude.

6. Let's say that you have decided to wear a tie. You pick a nice half-sleeve shirt and a matching tie. Take a look at the picture alongside and see how it looks. Doesn't quite make the mark, does it? Wearing a tie with a half-sleeve shirt is odd. Instead, a full-sleeved shirt and rolled-up sleeves looks smarter.

7. Sometimes, you stand next to someone and find that you can hardly breathe. The overwhelming smell of perfume is an instant put-off. You may smell good but remember to keep it mild. Some

people find heavy smells repulsive, some get a headache and others are allergic to certain strong smells. Therefore, use fragrances judiciously.

8. Wearing white socks with dark grey trousers and brown shoes could look strikingly odd. Wearing dark socks with dark-coloured clothing is more apt. The man should ideally be wearing black shoes and darker grey socks.

9. Denims are not really formal wear, but it is acceptable in certain semi-formal situations. Wearing denims with a formal shirt, blazer and casual shoes creates a confusing image and should be avoided.

10. Unkempt moustache and beard is unacceptable. This is very important as your face draws most of the attention. An unkempt beard, oily or unkempt hair, and moustache could mean several things but not formal. Make sure you trim or clean shave.

11. Picking the right footwear. The one that fits all is not correct. You could use different footwear at day and night. Your feet should be covered. Also, make sure that you keep the colours coordinated for a complete look. Remember, the colour of your shoes and belt should match, and avoid wearing white sports socks with formal wear.

'A woman can be overdressed but never over elegant'
Coco Chanel

Oftentimes, working women don't seem to have a rule book to follow when it comes to dressing. Instead, cultural influences, personal choices and preferences that come into play for them. Even so, there are a few common mistakes that women make while dressing for work.

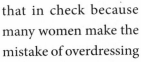

1. Delving too deep into fashion. Are you someone who loves to dress up? Well, keep that in check because  many women make the mistake of overdressing for office. The clothes that you wear could be in line with the latest fashion trend, but it may not be suitable for the workplace.

2. Over-accessorizing. This is not a crime but imagine walking into

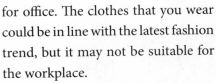

your workplace with chunky, noisy jewellery that shine too much. You may have achieved a great look clothes-wise, but you may have overdone the jewellery and accessories. The result may not be so pleasant. When wearing Indian attire especially, one must be careful to not over accessorize.

3. Wearing the wrong undergarments. We all may have fallen victim to this at some point. It is very important to choose correct lingerie as wearing the wrong type can ruin your attire and create awkward situations. There are clothing shops that offer free fitting sessions and help you pick out the correct undergarments.

4. Sporting heavy make-up. Make-up is essential nowadays but don't go overboard with it. Obvious lip-liner, too much foundation and concealer can be distinctly seen, and is distracting to others. Keep it simple and elegant.

5. Too much bling. Try not to divert attention to the unimportant elements of your attire. For example, avoid a bag or a watch that does not complement your clothes. Remember to retain focus where important.

6. Pay attention to colours. You do not have to stick to bland colours just because you are going to work. Play around with colours that complement each other and your natural

skin tone. Match elements of your clothes to form an impressive theme.

7. Hairstyles. Do you prefer the messy look? Well, it's not for work. Style your hair well and always keep it clean, neat and appropriate. However, there are a few blunders that you may

want to steer clear of, such as too much oil in the hair or decorating your hair with too many flowers that decay through the day. These are major put-offs especially when you are working in close quarters.

8. Pay attention to your nails. Chipped nails, fading nail polish and dirty fingernails are not just wrong; it shows poor standards of hygiene.

9. Picking the right footwear. The one that fits all is not correct. You could use different footwear at day and night. Let me ask you a question here. Would you wear peep-toe heels to office? Yes? That would be wrong. Your feet should be covered. Also, make sure that you keep the colours coordinated for a complete look.

POINTS TO NOTE

✓ The word 'power' in power dressing implies that an individual dresses to highlight their position of importance.

✓ Power dressing is a term that was originally intended for women.

✓ 1920s brought a new era in fashion with the Coco Chanel suit.

✓ You must dress to represent something. Therefore, you must dress for the audience, the setting, the culture, the company and yourself.

THREE

THE FOUR LEVELS OF DRESSING

WHY IS DRESSING CATEGORIZED into different levels? When we talk about formal dressing, doesn't it mean wearing a suit? Not exactly! Levels of clothing essentially mean the different levels of formal wear for men and women. For example, formal wear for men does not have to mean a black suit with tie and shoes. There are many levels of dressing that are appropriate for different situations and occasions. Let's take a look at the levels of clothing for men. This has been adapted from the Style Scale by Judith Rasband.

Level 1 or **Akasmik** dressing.

This level is meant for casual situations where a round or V-neck T-shirt, chinos or casual pants will be appropriate. However, are these good for the workplace? There is often

confusion as to where level 1 is applicable. How about a weekend lunch with colleagues, a post-work party or a casual meeting? You may not be at office, but you will still look semi-formal.

Level 2 or **Sadharan** dressing. At this level, you wear a full-sleeved shirt, a formal pant, a belt, shoes and you may or may not choose to wear a tie, but you will not wear a blazer. In India, you will often find this to be the most common office attire for men. This outfit would be ideal for a normal day at work.

Level 3 or **Peshawar** dressing. This level brings us the un-matte suit. It is characterized by contrast colours. For example, wearing a grey formal pant, a dark blue shirt and a dark blazer would have you representing level 3 of dressing. Level 3 can be built from level 2 by simply adding a blazer. It is great for meetings, client visits, office parties, etc.

Level 4 or **Aupacharik** dressing. The highest level of formal wear is the matte suit. This includes wearing the same colour pant and blazer with a

Level of Dressing	Cues	Men Indian	Men Western
Akasmik	round necks		
Sadharan	no coat or blazer		
Peshawar	Contrast suit		
Aupacharik	Matching suit		

Women Indian (Saree)	Women Indian (Salwar)	Women Western (Skirt)	Women Western (Trousers)

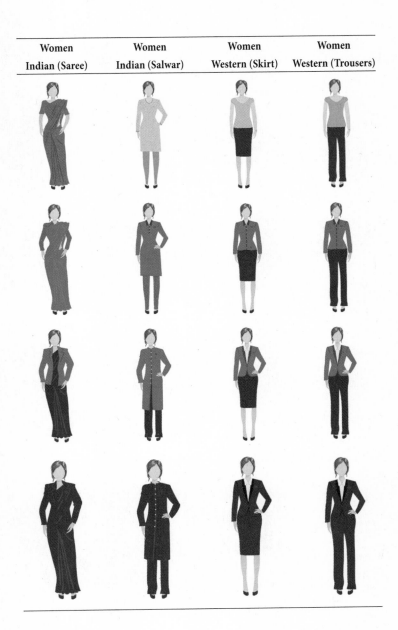

light-coloured shirt. For example, a classic black suit with a white shirt. It also involves coordinating all the other elements of your attire and attaining a uniformed look. You will find politicians, bureaucrats and top business people customarily dressed like this. Although this is the most authoritative level, it is not suitable for all occasions.

An everyday professional look for men ideally constitutes a shirt or T-shirt and pants with matching belt and shoes. While adding a tie, you should not only make sure that you coordinate it with your attire but keep in mind the knot. A well-knotted tie has a perfect triangle.

Even at level 1 of dressing, casual footwear must be avoided. Sneaker, sandals, floaters and shoes with worn-out heels are clearly non-business. Similarly, wearing socks that are uncoordinated, such as ones with patterns or multi-coloured stripes, are incorrect.

How about women? In terms of levels, the same logic applies for them too. However, you will find that women seem to have a lot more options considering that we will talk about appropriate Indian wear for each level too.

Level 1. The casual level can constitute jeans and a good fabric top. Add minimalistic accessories and you are done. If you want to wear Indian attire, then a simple salwar kameez or a saree works well.

Level 2. A semi-casual look with contrast pants or skirt and a shirt would complete level 2. For the Indian look, you can try a formal kurti and pant, or a classic saree pinned at the shoulder.

Level 3. Level 3 is un-matte for ladies as well. A contrast suit, either pants or skirt, with a blazer is ideal. For an Indian touch, you can experiment with a straight-cut kurti and pants of the same colour, and add a long jacket or stole. You could also wear a saree and add a contrasting blazer to it.

Level 4. A matte suit of the same colour with a pant or a skirt represents level 4. If you are going for Indian wear, your kurta and pant must be of the same colour with a colour coordinated stole or jacket. Even if you choose to wear a saree, you must ensure that the colour of your saree and blazer are the same. As for men, uniformity is the essence of level 4.

Since there is more variety in women's attire, they should be careful with their selections. Even as casual wear, tops with too many frills and ruffles, transparent or translucent layers, awkward shapes and clothes with large elements

must be avoided. Footwear must be well-coordinated and appropriate to the setting. For example, wearing closed shoes with heels to work in the morning and wearing short pencil heel stilettos for a party at night would be great. Heels are a good choice for any occasion but having the right pair and matching it with your clothes is essential. Platform heels, peep-toes, colourful slippers and untidy sandals are definite image killers.

Women also have an array of choices with their handbags. Plain or reptile leather bags in angular shapes are highly recommended. For professional occasions, a structured formal handbag is the ideal choice. With corporate dressing constantly undergoing changes, the appropriate wear for any occasion is debatable. This is where image consultants come in – to keep you up-to-date with the latest trends.

POINTS TO NOTE

✓ Level 4 of dressing is the matte suit.
✓ Level 3 of dressing is the un-matte suit.
✓ Level 2 of dressing involves semi-formal outfits.
✓ Level 1 of dressing involves casual wear.

FOUR

DRESSING FOR YOUR BODY SHAPE

HOW OFTEN DO WE think of our body shapes while dressing or shopping? I often like tops that I know will not flatter my body shape at all, but I end up convincing myself to buy them. Then, later I accept that it doesn't actually look good on me or go with my other outfits. As a result, such tops and clothes just pile up in my wardrobe. I decided to take charge and stop.

It is true that certain shapes, patterns and colours are far more suitable for one body shape than the other. Understanding our body shapes thus becomes important. Picking clothes that flatter your shape and are complementary to each other is challenging, no doubt, but it helps create a better, more classic silhouette.

For example, if you have a wide hip and a larger lower body as compared to your upper body, certain types of clothing may not look appropriate, such as wearing a short top with tight jeans or a short dress. Try and draw attention away from areas we would like to camouflage.

Often, we simply look at our body according to its horizontal width and categorize ourselves into the common types of body shapes. However, mind that you must determine your vertical body type, the shape of your face, your height and weight, your bone structure, shoulders and take note of your problem areas while categorizing your body shape. So, there is quite a lot to consider!

This chapter aims to discuss the different body shapes for men and women. You will find each shape named differently for men as well as women and you have an image counsel that will advise you on the best course of action, to help you dress effectively. Try them out!

TYPES OF BODY SHAPES FOR MEN

The types of body shapes that I have listed are not exhaustive or the only list available. In order to keep this simple and easy to follow, I have stuck to a list of five. A good exercise while reading would be to try and identify which category you belong to.

1. The Congruent

The congruent body shape has broad shoulders and a broad chest with the body line gently tapering towards the

np

waist and legs. If you fall under this category, you can pretty much try any style, shape and pattern. Clothing experts would consider this figure the easiest to style as almost anything would suit you.

What the image counsel says: Your frame can see you experimenting with sleek athletic wear, slim-fit shirts, trousers and even jumpers and sneakers.

2. The Body Builder

This type of body shape denotes large shoulders and chest that are significantly broader than the waist. Although you are closer to the congruent body shape, those in this category should focus on building up their midriffs and waists, and reducing their upper bodies.

What the image counsel says: V-neck T-shirts, slim-fit shirts, straight trousers and horizontal stripes would suit this shape the best. Horizontal stripes especially on the shirt can create an illusion of a wider waist to match your upper body. Patterned trousers or shorts are also great for the body builder. Cottons and fine wools are your go-to fabrics.

Steer clear from well-fitted suits, especially ones with shoulder padding. Also, avoid creative necklines, prints and patterns on the chest and shoulders. The body builder shape should focus on taking attention away from the upper part of the body.

3. The Homologous

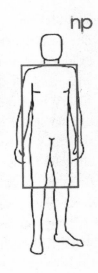

The homologous man is proportionate in a way that the body shape would seem like two parallel vertical lines. The idea here should be to create a structure for your body. This, of course, provides leeway for experimentation with various structures.

What the image counsel says: Horizontal stripes, especially across the upper body, are best for you. Tailored suits with padded shoulders, layered clothing, scarves and ties can give a bulk effect to your chest. Also, prints and colours on the shirt can draw much needed attention to a structured upper body.

It is best to avoid double-breasted jackets, rectangular suits and shirts as these will do nothing to add structure to your figure.

4. The Convex

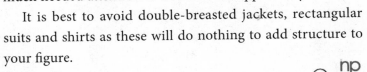

The convex body shape is characterized by a large waist and hip compared to other parts of the body. This shape typically represents a closed bracket – (). While this doesn't necessarily mean that you are in bad shape, it could mean that you will have a tougher time finding appropriate clothing.

What the image counsel says: Try vertical stripes that help elongate your body and give a more petite midriff. Jackets with a refined shoulder line could do wonders. Checked blazers or a well-fitted waistcoat can make you look more balanced. Go for brighter colours with details on the chest, and also experiment with wool-blends and linen in multiple drapes.

Try to avoid a fuller look, especially if you are on the heavier side. Keep tight polo shirts and turtle necks at bay as they draw attention to your waist. Bulky and bling belts can also pull focus onto the waist area. Similarly, skinny-fit jeans that taper down often give a pronounced convex effect.

5. The Spherical

True to its name, this represents a rounded or circular body shape. Although a sphere shape appears most rounded around the waist, the rest of the body is relatively similar in size. The best way to dress is to enlarge your shoulder area and focus on a tapering effect chest-down.

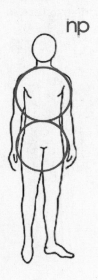

What the image counsel says: Vertical stripes are the go-to if you want to look slimmer. Adorn pinstripe shirts and trousers. Vertically patterned fabrics without ruffles and folds will give your limbs an elongated look. Your trousers should ideally be straight fit and a bit loose to give structure. Stick to stiff and solid fabrics. The goal is to create a structure so that the problem areas are aptly covered.

Keep away from horizontal stripes. They will simply give an impression of a wide girth. Don't opt for contrast colours unless they are distributed proportionately. Bulky belts, double-breasted suits, and excessive fabric concentration in particular parts of the body can have you looking stout. If you are short, avoid boots as they take away height.

TYPES OF BODY SHAPES FOR WOMEN

Body shapes for women usually outnumber those for men. On the Internet, you will find twelve to fifteen body shapes for women. However, I feel the four broad shapes discussed below can sufficiently accommodate each and every one of you ladies.

An interesting point about the four shapes that I have listed below is that their names correspond to the various chakras in the body. Visuddha is the throat representing a pear shape, Ajna is the third eye that represents a rectangular figure, Manipura is the solar plexus denoting the apple shape and Anahata is the heart, which represents the hourglass figure.

I hope you find my image counsel particularly interesting as these simple solutions are all you need to be equipped with for your next shopping trip.

1. The Pear – Visuddha

This figure has a wide lower body with a rounded bottom and a defined waist line. In comparison, your upper body will look lean, which therefore becomes your focus area. Adding volume to your shoulders and torso will help balance your shape.

What the image counsel says: Experiment with necklines to accentuate the shoulders; slim the hip and thighs with interesting patterns and hems like a high-low top or tulip skirt. Jackets and ruffled sleeves can also add a nice appeal. Try A-line skirts and pair dark-coloured bottoms with light-coloured tops. Give yourself some height with classy heels.

Tight-fitted trousers with crop tops, skinny jeans, straight skirts and short dresses are likely to attract focus onto the problem areas and it is best to avoid these.

2. The Tube or Rectangle – Ajna

Similar to parallel lines, the waist, hip and shoulders will be around the same size in width. If you belong here, show off your hands and legs more to create structure. Your focus must be to make a structure for yourself by creating curves and highlighting your limbs.

What the image counsel says: Crop tops and skirts can be your best friends. Feel free to accessorize and use belts to pull the waist in. A long skirt with a side slit can help draw attention to your legs. Similarly, short sleeves and accessories on your hand can direct focus there. Plan and layer your clothes well.

Try not to overindulge and wear too many styles. A-line jackets and straight dresses may have you looking further parallel.

3. The Apple – Manipura

With slender and narrow hips, women in this shape have a defined and strong upper body. The back, chest and shoulders are broad giving the waist and legs a tapering look. You need to bring the focus on your legs and create an illusion of an elongated upper body.

What the image counsel says: Your staples should include V-necks and A-lines. Create structure at your waist to get maximum attention there. Bulky belts, jackets and structured tops will fit the bill. Try creating a curve at the hips and streamline the torso. Boot-cut pants and short skirts can be great for you.

Avoid polychromatic looks and stiff tops. Underplay the shoulders and avoid padded jackets and shoulder pads.

4. The Hourglass – Anahata

Said to be the ideal body shape, it is characterized by the hips and shoulders being proportionate, with a narrow waist. Since your body is naturally curvaceous, fitting clothes to match your shape is the best strategy. Your goal is to show off your natural figure.

What the image counsel says: Strike a fine balance. Maintain the proportions of your hips and torso, and fine tune the waistline – avoid wearing clothes that give an illusion of a narrower waist. That makes the body looks disproportionate. Fitted tops that hug the waist will complement your figure well. V-necks, belts, A-line cuts and shaped dresses are all suitable for you. You will look great in high waist skirts, skinny jeans and wrap dresses.

Make sure not to hide your curves behind straight cut, loose and baggy outfits. The jersey material could be your enemy as it hugs every curve or problem area. Select good fabrics and minimalistic patterns to make the best of your gifts.

'The dress must follow the body of a woman, not the body following the shape of the dress' Hubert de Givenchy

POINTS TO NOTE

- ✓ The congruent body shape for men is characterized by broad shoulders and a broad chest with the body line gently tapering towards the waist and legs.
- ✓ The body builder shape for men denotes large shoulders and chest that are significantly broader than the waist.
- ✓ The homologous body shape for men is proportionate in a way that the body shape seems like two parallel lines. The idea here should be to create a structure for your body.
- ✓ The convex body shape for men is characterized by a large waist and hip compared to other parts of the body. This shape typically represents a closed bracket – ().

✓ The sphere shape is most rounded around the waist, the rest of the body is similar in size.

✓ The Visuddha shape for women refers to a wide lower body with a rounded bottom and a defined waistline.

✓ The Ajna shape for women is similar to two parallel lines where the waist, hip and shoulders will be around the same size in width.

✓ The Manipura body shape for women is characterized by slender and narrow hips with a defined and strong upper body. The back, chest and shoulders are broad giving the waist and legs a tapering look.

✓ The Anahata body shape for women is said to be the ideal body shape. It is characterized by the hips and shoulders being proportionate and a narrow waist.

* Adapted from the International Style Scale.

FIVE

THE WORKING WOMAN

THIS CHAPTER IS A short story about a woman, Sunita Sharma, who is at a senior management level at her firm. The story will also act as a recall exercise for you. Over the past four chapters, you may have understood quite a bit about the dos and don'ts of dressing and its impact on your image. Try finding out what Sunita is doing right or wrong in terms of her dressing while reading through the story.

BUSINESS ATTIRE FOR WOMEN

Sunita Verma is the Managing Director of YOQ Corp. Being the senior-most member of the company, she only reports to the chairman and shareholders. This definitely puts her in a critically influential position, not just with regard to work but even in other ways. Although she is not questioned by anyone, she walks into office by 9 a.m. sharp. She is very organized and sticks to a pre-planned schedule. She is always immaculately dressed in branded clothes. Her employees have never seen her wearing anything casual. Recently, the annual report conference saw her making a presentation about the company's performance. Many of her employees were smitten by the way she carried herself. She wore her straight hair loose with a knee-length skirt, shirt and a designer blazer.

Her shirt was plain white, paired with a ruffled white straight-cut skirt. A sky-blue blazer that had three buttons completed her attire. She also wore her favourite white peep-toe heels. Since the previous chapter spoke about dressing for your body shape, let me also give you an idea about Sunita's body shape. Her body shape is typically Visuddha with a lower body that is significantly larger than her upper body. She is also quite tall for an Indian woman, around 5"7'.

Try to picture Sunita and analyze the right and wrong aspects of her dressing while keeping in mind her body shape.

First, try to recall the levels of dressing, at which level would you categorize Sunita's outfit at the presentation? Did you think of level 3? That would be correct. Now, let's analyze her outfit. Her choices in terms of colour seem fine. A plain white shirt is classic and a blue blazer with it is great.

You might have guessed the problem areas here – the skirt and the heels. Even if it is a straight cut, knee-length skirt, ruffled ones are not formal wear. It attracts a lot of undesirable attention. Also, if her lower body is larger compared to her upper body, ruffles will add to the volume making her look further disproportionate. Had the ruffles been on her blazer or sleeves, it would have helped her achieve a balanced look.

Secondly, peep-toes or open heel shoes are generally not formal. Sunita is a tall woman and does not need to add more height. She can use smaller heels that are covered, and a more formal option.

It is important to remember that even if you like branded clothing, making it situation-appropriate and considering your body shape is essential.

ACCESSORIES FOR WOMEN

Now that Sunita Verma's example has given you an idea about how your clothes and footwear can portray your image, let's consider the other elements or rather accessories that women often wear. Although there are no wrong accessories, there are some that are more desirable than others in a corporate setting.

Remember not to wear clashing accessories that take away attention from your face. For example, a pair of chunky earrings could have people constantly noticing them rather than your presentation. Similarly, if you wear big hooped earrings with a heavy necklace, both will contradict each other giving you a very unprofessional look.

Here are a few tips to help you pick out the right accessories.
1. Earrings – Stick to simple small shapes that don't overpower your face. Even if it is made of precious metal,

it should merely be an addition to the overall look and not the primary focus. Which is why you should ideally avoid hoops or dangling earrings, and ones that make noise or ones that are too shiny.

2. Sunglasses – Golden-coloured sunglasses are most preferred, followed by silver and tortoise shell. Avoid big and decorated frames that touch your brow line and tinted lenses.

3. Scarves – They are a classic accessory that look great when worn appropriately. Scarves can well be considered as a tie for women. Square-shaped scarves are better than oblong ones because they are more formal. In terms of material, go for silk scarves. Chiffon and cotton should be your last preferences because these fabrics are not as formal as silk.

4. Other jewellery – Even if you love wearing jewellery, a minimalistic approach is most elegant. Diamonds and pearls are most formal, followed by gold, silver and gold-silver mix. Indians are considerably fonder of gold, but it would be wise to avoid too much shine. If you are fond of rings, wear just one ring per hand.

5. Watch – Your wrist watch can be golden, silver or metallic.
   A watch with bracelet-style strap is most elegant.

IMAGE BREAKERS

We have discussed 'what to do' all through the previous chapters. It's time to learn about a few important image breakers.

So, what are image breakers? Elements of your image that are particularly awkward and make the people around you uncomfortable are called image breakers.

Paying attention to avoid image breakers can do a lot for your image. Some of the most common image breakers for women are listed below.

- Chipped nail polish on your finger nails or toe nails that are easily visible.
- Applying too much make-up so that your face is a different colour compared to the rest of your skin.
- Stained or yellow teeth.
- Poorly maintained hair with too much oil or fragrant flowers.
- A major focus area that women should also pay great attention to is their undergarments. You will be surprised that many women get this wrong. Inappropriate ones could make your clothes look awkward and make people around you uncomfortable. Nowadays, it shouldn't be hard to pick out appropriate innerwear as several lingerie shops offer free trials to check your size and help find the correct undergarments. Similarly, don't wear clothes that are too tight or too baggy.
- Footwear that expose your heels, especially if they are cracked. This will show that you do not invest time in taking care of yourself.
- Most importantly, make sure that you take measures to avoid body odour. Use mild perfumes and deodorants

especially towards the end of a day when the fragrance that you applied in the morning might have lost effect.

- An additional tip that people often forget is to use a mouth freshener, especially after eating pungent food. If your mouth smells foul, it will definitely make your colleagues stay away and create an even worse impression on important clients.

'Create your own style. Let it be unique for yourself and identifiable for others' Anna Wintour

SIX

THE WORKING MAN

JUST LIKE WE HAD 'The Working Woman' as a recall example for you, let's try having one for the working man as well. The following short story will describe Ravi's dressing style, his body shape and three situations that he finds himself in. Try figuring out if his dressing is appropriate for each of the situations below and what he has done right or wrong.

BUSINESS ATTIRE FOR MEN

Ravi is the co-founder and one of the director's at PNN Bearings Ltd. The company manufactures ball bearings and is leading in the automotive industry. Ravi's position requires him to meet several people throughout the day. He talks to his colleagues at work, he meets many of his clients and partners to propel the business, he maintains a progressive relationship with shareholders and tries to be a link among various teams and departments at work. Thus, his job requires him to constantly make presentations, speeches, have discussions and interact. He has his plate full but enjoys it all.

Ravi is tall and well-built. He loves to spend free time at the gym building muscle. His physique resembles that of a body builder's. Take a look at the situations below and see what you can find.

Situation 1 – On one particular Monday, Ravi had scheduled a meeting with two of the shareholders of the company. It was an important meeting that was to be held in a conference room at one of the hotels nearby. Ravi was wearing a dark blue blazer with dark blue formal pants. He wore a white shirt and a classic brown belt. He made sure to wear black-grey combination socks with black shoes. He looked at himself and felt confident.

Is something wrong with Ravi's dressing? You may have remembered the thumb rule that was stated earlier. Your belt and shoes must always be of the same colour. In this case, Ravi should have gone for a plain black belt instead of a brown one.

Situation 2 – Ravi was in a meeting with two of his friends who also happened to be the vice president and a team leader in the company. The meeting was also attended by the VP's executive assistant, Ravi's secretary and a few team members from the marketing department. It was an in-house meeting and he didn't have to make a presentation. Ravi was wearing a black shirt with cream pants. He also wore black shoes and a black belt. The only accessory he had on was his silver watch. He had just smoked a cigarette before coming into the meeting.

His clothes seem appropriate for the meeting. Do you think the smoking may have been the problem here? Absolutely right! The problem is that Ravi had created an image breaker. He had walked into the meeting right after having a smoke. Being in a small closed room, everyone could smell the odour of tobacco on Ravi. He shook hands with a few people in the room and the odour passed onto their hands too. This is a very serious image breaker as it causes discomfort to many, especially those who do not smoke.

Situation 3 – The office had organized an annual party at one of the elite clubs one night. Ravi was planning to go there directly after work. He decided to be formal and wore a full black ensemble: a black blazer with padded shoulders, a black shirt, black socks and shoes and a black belt. His silver watch was the only non-black item on him.

What do you think about this situation? Does Ravi look great? He definitely does! However, for an after-work party, isn't Ravi a tad overdressed? He could easily go for a high-profile meeting with potential clients wearing the same outfit. His formal demeanour could portray a serious image to his colleagues at the party. So, his colleagues are likely to perceive him as closed and unapproachable. You must remember that although level 4 is considered most formal, it is not appropriate everywhere.

There is another small imperfection here. Did you notice the padded shoulders? Having a physique like a body builder, Ravi should try to take attention away from his chest and shoulders. With his padded-shoulder blazer, Ravi looks even more pumped up making his waist and legs look further tapered; a disproportionate figure.

ACCESSORIES FOR MEN

When it comes to accessories for men, there is unfortunately not enough to experiment with, especially in corporate dressing. However, this also makes things easy for you as there isn't much that you can do to go terribly wrong.

1. Watch – Often, men don't have too many options for accessories on their hand. Considering that it is usually a single piece of watch, invest on a classy one. Metallic watches are the best but you could also try black or brown leather straps.

2. Tie – Your tie should coordinate with your attire and have a perfect knot. Also, your tie should end right above your trousers; not too long, not too short. Make sure that you buy ones that complement most of your clothes. Silk ties are the best. Choose the patterns and colours carefully. A blue silk tie is most preferable

3. Belt – Experiment with leather and reptile pattern belts in basic colours – black and brown. Mind the sizes as you do not want your belt to be too wide or too narrow or too long.

4. Shoes – Leather shoes are a must. Blacks and browns are classic and you can choose between with lace or without. Most formal shoes come with a certain amount of height from the heel of the shoe. What you  should focus on most is the shape of the toes. Cap-toes and plain toes are classic. Don't opt for square or extremely elongated toes

IMAGE BREAKERS

Most people do not know that there are certain aspects of their behaviour or personality that are major image breakers. For example, you are attending a meeting at office and you keep chewing gum. Not only is it going to be distracting to the others, it is considered bad manners to constantly chew in a professional setting. The degree of image breakers varies depending on their seriousness. There are some that are far worse than others. Take a look at a few image breakers for men.

1. Hair – In this case, it is not just your beard and moustache that needs maintenance, you must also ensure that you don't have protruding nasal hair. Pay attention and regularly trim nasal hair to avoid a major image breaker.

2. Bad breath – As much as chewing gum is undesirable, having bad breath is equally poor. It can have people

running in the opposite direction from you. If you tend to have bad breath, especially after having a pungent meal, use a mouth freshener or quickly brush your teeth.

3. Body odour – This is a major point of concern for most men and it could also be one of the worst image breakers. It is difficult to smell great all through a nine-hour work day. You may be prone to perspiring or your job may involve working outdoors. Therefore, keep perfumes or deodorants handy.

4. Tight clothes and underwear show – With the right-sized clothes, you should be able to stand, sit and breathe comfortably. If your clothes squeeze you as soon as you sit, you are wearing the wrong size. This can be awkward and the discomfort can be distracting. Similarly, if you are wearing casual jeans or trousers that are loose, ensure that you are not offering others a peak of your underwear. It is not a pleasant sight and it shows carelessness.

5. Stained teeth – Rinse your mouth after eating meals and before meeting people. Visit a dentist if you think your teeth are no longer white and are showing tints of yellow. If you are a smoker, there is a greater chance of your teeth turning yellowish.

6. Long nails – Unkempt, long and dirty nails are hygiene issues. Since your hands are easily visible and you may have to offer a handshake at some point, people will notice your nails and their untidiness. Worst case, you may even end up poking someone. Keeping your nails trim and tidy is part of personal hygiene, which says a lot about you.

7. Dirty shoes – It is often said that people judge another person's social status by merely looking at the shoes that he is wearing. Your shoes can reveal a lot about you. Therefore, do not wear old and worn out shoes, shoes that don't have a good sole or, especially, shoes that haven't been cleaned and polished.

'You can have anything you want if you dress for it'
Edith Head

SEVEN

SKINCARE AND PERSONAL GROOMING TECHNIQUES

POWER DRESSING IS A complete package. It takes into account not just the clothes you wear, but also the rest of your appearance. Skincare and personal grooming are as important as dressing well and other aspects of one's image. In fact, proper grooming takes the unnecessary spotlight away from you, allowing people to focus on the essentials of what you are saying. It also allows people to get to know the real you. Personal grooming done right tells people what you think about yourself. Now, skincare and personal grooming are not only for women. Men must commit to taking care of themselves as well.

Skincare regimens can be different for men and women considering that there are vast differences between the two. For men, using a good face wash, shampoo and body wash, hair gel, a shaving kit, cologne and other fragrances are imperative. Women may have more requirements when it comes to haircare including shampoo, conditioners, hair sprays and serums. Skincare can include a range of creams and moisturizers, sunscreen, make-up items, etc. Also, perfumes and deodorants are important components.

It is impossible to generalize what men or women must do to maintain their skin because each individual is different and has different requirements. You must figure out what skin type you have and what kind of products suit you. Especially those with sensitive skin and those prone to skin ailments must consult a dermatologist.

STYLING

Each person can create his or her own style. However, this step comes after you have achieved a good sense of the basics in dressing and grooming. It must be kept in mind that style statements at work must not collide with casual fashion as that does not fall under power dressing.

Men can experiment with suits, colours and patterns to be safe. The current trending style is to take inspiration from the bygone years. Look to the '70s, '80s and '90s, and try to recreate it by adding your own style. Gelled hairstyles may be good too but don't overdo them with too much gel or Mohawks.

When it comes to experimenting, women may be the luckier lot. You can try a number of hairstyles and accessories. Experiment with your clothes and you too should look at the '90s for inspiration.

For every good look that is achieved, there is quite a bit of effort that goes into it. If you want to look great, you must invest time and effort to discover your own style and portray it elegantly. Take the time to care for yourself, your skin, hair, appearance and groom your personality. In a global workplace, these will be sure to catch an eye as much as your work does.

HAIRSTYLES

The important thing is to follow a few basic principles each time you try a new hairstyle. First, keep it simple; second, keep it neat; and third, be versatile. If your hairstyle adheres to these principles, you will always get it right. While styling your hair, you must also keep the shape of your face and your clothes in mind. Just as you dress differently for each occasion, your hairstyle must complement your dressing for each occasion. Let's start with a few hairstyles for men.

1. The classic taper cut

This is also called the businessman's haircut. It never goes out of fashion.

2. Side partitioned, slicked back

A good hair product may be advisable to achieve this look. It is a traditional look that is back in fashion.

3. Crew cut

A spin-off of the popular army cut, the crew cut is very short. For those who like to keep it short, this may be ideal.

4. Ivy league haircut

This is a longer version of the crew cut. It almost always includes a side partition and is classic.

Now, let's look at a few hairstyles for women.

1. Classic ponytail

This is a neat and low-maintenance option as it gives you no reason for constant adjustment. It also looks professional.

2. Low bun

A low bun is a very professional look although it may have you looking a bit older. However, it also conveys authority.

3. Braids

Braids are a perfect combination of professional and relaxed as they are suitable for the workplace and for casual wear.

4. Fringes and bangs

Fringes and bangs are not suitable for all faces. Also, they can give a very casual look if not well-maintained or trimmed regularly.

5. Short hair

There are multiple haircuts you can get if you like it short. It is definitely easier to maintain and can give you a neat look.

Hairstyles for the workplace

MAKE-UP

'If you're sad, add more lipstick and attack' Coco Chanel

A lot of women apply make-up and there are those who don't. If you want to know which is better in a professional setting, let's say you must have some make-up on. It could be an essential part of completing your look. A few basic make-up tips can help us kick start this topic.

First, do some research on your skin type, skin colour and make-up colours that will go with your skin tone. What make-up does is provide texture and colour to your skin that could otherwise look plain and monotonous.

Second, use the necessary products to prep your skin before diving into application. Remember, how well you ready your skin for make-up can determine its longevity and look.

Third, always keep a few touch-ups items with you for sudden meetings or presentations as your make-up is most likely to fade through the day.

There is a particular sequence of applying make-up. It starts with getting your skin ready and then following a pattern. Going step-by-step is actually a time saver and gets you the right look. Here are the steps for your reference:

a) Cleaning
b) Concealing
c) Foundation
d) Compact
e) Eyes
f) Blush
g) Lip
h) Hair

Cleaning – Give your face a nice wash and apply moisturizer. The best way to start is by making your skin clean and supple.

Concealing – Concealers are used primarily if you have spots and blemishes that you want to cover. Conceal the problem areas carefully so that they don't form a blotch on your face. To blend well, use a concealer brush.

Foundation – Picking the right foundation is imperative. Your foundation should be as close as possible to your natural skin tone. This must be applied to your face, neck and ears as you want all these areas to have an even look. Use a brush to apply your foundation, especially if it is liquid.

Compact – Compact sets everything in place and gives it a finishing touch. For those with oily skin, keeping a compact handy will help to keep the shine off through the day when touching up.

Eyes – Eye make-up can be a defining factor on your face. A few essentials are eye pencil, eye liner, mascara and eye shadow. For the most formal look, use black pencil and liner, and light pastel shades of eye shadow. However, try different looks for different occasions. In order of application, apply your eye shadow first, the eye pencil second, eye liner comes third, and finally finish it with light mascara. Do not overdo your eyes with too many colours, thick liner or wings unless it is a party.

Blush – Blush should always look smoothly blended with your skin for a natural appearance. If you apply too much, you will have two circles on your cheeks, while too little will be almost invisible. Use a soft brush and smile while applying to achieve the perfect look.

Lip – Use a lip liner to add an outline to your lips and fill in with lipstick. Make sure your lip liner and lipstick are of the same shade to achieve uniformity. Don't let you lip liner stand out in comparison to your lipstick. Maroons, magentas, pinks and light reds are ideal for business.

Hair – Always do your hair after you have finished applying make-up. Ensure that you haven't applied products to your hairline and always keep your hair tied back when applying make-up.

Despite doing everything perfectly, you must remember that a natural glow is always the best look. To achieve that, you must maintain your body and skin from within. Drink a lot of water as keeping yourself hydrated is best for your skin. Eat greens, seasonal fruits and nuts in abundance. Eating right gives your skin a young and beautiful glow.

FRAGRANCES

Men and women have varied preferences and choices when it comes to fragrances. Indisputably, all must smell pleasant at work to maintain a good image. Not doing so is one of the worst image breakers. You can use deodorants on your skin and perfume on your clothes. It is often said that wearing perfume on your neck and wrists, at the pulse points, make an impact far better than wearing perfume under your arms or elsewhere.

Fragrances that are most suitable for women include floral or sweet, chypre or citrus, spicy, woody, oriental exotic and musk tones. Fragrances that are most suitable for men include spicy, citrus, clean, musk and earthy tones.

The most important thing to note while wearing perfume to work is that you mustn't overdo it. Especially in closed spaces, strong smells circulate and not everyone is comfortable with strong smells. So, make sure that you smell good when people are in close contact with you but that should be the limit.

PERSONAL HYGIENE

Personal hygiene is all-encompassing. It primarily includes your basic hygiene but also takes into account grooming (hair, skin and clothes), dressing and self-maintenance. Getting ready for work should therefore be a process: taking a shower, wearing fresh clothes, setting your hair, applying make-up (for women), wearing nice accessories, picking shoes, a good bag, using a good deodorant or perfume. While you go through your daily rituals, make sure to have checkpoints to ensure that you are avoiding dangerous image breakers. Men should check if their facial hair is well-groomed, their clothes are in good condition, shoes are polished etc. Women must ensure that their hair and make-up are done right, that their clothes and accessories are appropriate and that they have taken care of their manicure and pedicure needs.

How you take care of yourself speaks volumes about your personality and the importance that you give to your work. A hygienic person is automatically assumed to be more organized in life and at work. So, your personal hygiene standards can rub off on many other aspects, creating an impression about you.

POINTS TO NOTE

✓ Create your own style keeping in mind a few basic principles.

✓ Keep your hairstyles simple, neat and versatile.
✓ Don't apply too much make-up or too little, and follow a step-by-step method for application.
✓ Use fragrances to smell good but never overdo it.
✓ Personal hygiene is very important as it encompasses grooming, dressing and self-maintenance.

EIGHT

POWER DRESSING GLOBALLY

MEETING CLIENTS FROM OTHER countries or visiting other countries for work makes power dressing doubly important. This is because each country has its own definition of power dressing with some being extremely formal, while others focusing more on casual. Always remember the phrase, 'When in Rome, do as the Romans do.' If you are to be taken seriously in a foreign setting, among people from a completely different culture, make sure that you do some research on their ways of dressing, and try to follow it in your own style.

For example, if you are in Italy and people there are not accustomed to wearing blazers even for meetings, you should avoid it too. Try to fit in or rather blend in, because people have an affinity for those who they think are like them. If you dress and present yourself like your colleague from another country, he or she is more likely to be fond of you owing to similarity. This approach could be very good for business as there are always things to talk about if you have something in common.

Although we can't cover all the countries in the world, let's take a look at few countries that we tend to associate with professionally on a regular basis.

AMERICA

Dress code for work varies in different parts of America. It also varies depending on your industry and your designation. For the most part, Americans are more relaxed and keen to experiment. If you are new, it is always best to start with a formal suit. Men wear blazers and ties. However, Americans

UNITED STATES OF AMERICA

are known to remove their blazers and jackets when indoors. Loosening the tie is also an American habit. They are particular about quality footwear and briefcases.

Women wear formal suits and dresses. They avoid flashy clothes and jewellery or too much make-up during the day. There are several offices that allow casual wear and you can see a wide variety of clothes being worn. So, check for place-specific business attire if you plan to visit the States.

GERMANY

Germans are known to be one of the most formal and conservative people when it comes to business wear. They also greatly value punctuality and organization. Men usually wear dark-coloured business suits with ties and white shirts. Women also wear dark-coloured suits and conservative

GERMANY

dresses. The dress code for work remains the same even if the weather is significantly warmer. Germans are not big fans of change and experimentation at the workplace. Therefore, women are encouraged to dress modestly with minimum make-up and accessories.

JAPAN

The Japanese share a lot in common with the Germans with regard to punctuality and organization. They are conservative when it comes to business wear and dress to impress. Ideally, men's wear consists of a good business suit preferably in dark colours. They also greatly value quality. Therefore, it would be wise to invest in an expensive, well-fitted suit. Unlike most other countries, Japanese women do not wear heels to work as it is considered inappropriate and they also avoid wearing

JAPAN

trousers. Business dresses or skirts with a blazer are thought to be ideal. Too many accessories or make-up are definitely not appreciated, and they are most comfortable sticking to simple and classic clothes.

UAE

The work culture in UAE is quite different from India. They work on Sundays because Fridays and Saturdays are holidays and most offices start by 8 a.m. In India, you increasingly find workplaces adopting a more casual culture. However, in a corporate office in the UAE, you are expected to be in proper formal attire, i.e., a suit or blazer. Your formal attire can be perceived to be incomplete without a tie. If you work at a senior management level, you will be expected to wear suits every day.

UNITED ARAB EMIRATES

Women are expected to be fully covered, especially in more conservative areas. Their traditional outfit of burqa is acceptable almost everywhere, but if you prefer western formals, make sure you avoid skirts, short dresses and low necklines.

FRANCE

The French are highly fashion conscious and you are likely to find even entry-level executives dressed immaculately. Men wear suits that are cut differently compared to the suits worn by men in other countries. They almost always wear a jacket and a tie, and do not remove their jackets at work as it is considered unprofessional. The French do not even loosen their tie as their American counterparts do.

Women are even more fashion conscious and are known to be up-to-date with formal and casual trends. Women wear

FRANCE

suits or dresses to work and a great deal of importance is given to footwear by both genders.

UK

The British are very particular and tend to identify themselves differently from others. They are definitely more conservative and formal compared to the Americans, but not as conservative as the Germans. A classic suit in blue or charcoal is best for Britain. Well-polished shoes are appreciated, and it is best to avoid striped ties here. Cuff links, pocket squares and the nitty-gritties of complete formal attire are well respected in the UK.

Women wear formal suits with trousers or skirts, and even conservative dresses. Coats and jackets are worn according to the weather and a good pair of heels is a necessity. There are

UNITED KINGDOM

set rules for business casuals as well but people do not show up in jeans or flip flops even then.

AUSTRALIA

Australians are friendly and open, but directness and brevity are valued. Management level businessmen wear dark suits and ties as a standard, while women wear business suits with either skirts or trousers. A casual attire is preferred if work happens outside the main cities. Known to be a hot country for much of the year, light-weight and cool clothing is recommended. Australians tend to avoid excessive jewellery as they may be perceived to be too flashy and unprofessional. Informal clothing is widely followed for non-business related meetings or events.

AUSTRALIA

CHINA

The Chinese have begun adopting a much more western style of dressing, especially in the commercial and urban areas. Many places are witnessing the exit of the traditional Mao jacket and trousers. It is recommended to carry smart business attire with you when visiting China. Men can wear plain suits in beige, brown or dark blue and ties that are not too flashy. Women can wear business formals that are not too western. High heels are not preferred by Chinese women, and neither are short-sleeves and low necklines. Revealing clothing is seen as in poor taste by them.

The Chinese give importance to appearance as they see it as an indicator of how successful you are. While it is not necessary to be over dressed, it is a good idea to wear good quality clothes and accessories if you are looking to create

CHINA

a first impression. Do not wear jeans for formal business meetings. Shorts or casual wear is preferred for sporting or non-business get togethers.

RUSSIA

Russians tend to dress well and spend most of their income on clothes. Men prefer a dark suit or a jacket with tie, trousers and polished shoes in order to create a good professional impression. Women wear conservative dress in general, but business suits or blouses and skirts are the preferred dressing style for business meetings. Russian women avoid flashy and gaudy outfits.

Standing with your hands inside your pockets in public is seen as rude behaviour in Russia. It is advisable not to wear costly accessories in public from a safety perspective.

RUSSIA

ITALY

The Italians are known for their fashion trends around the world. They have a natural flair for dressing well and at the same time, they compliment anyone who looks good. Good clothes are seen as a signature of success in all business meetings. Regardless of the industry, Italian professionals will invariably be well-groomed and wear good-quality attire.

Men wear fashionable, high-quality suits. While the shirts could be single-coloured or striped, it is a common practice to pair it with a designer tie. Women dress up in an elite manner for formal business meetings and slacks are not preferred by either sex. High quality leather belts, shoes and quality accessories elevate the impression you create while in Italy.

ITALY

POINTS TO NOTE

✓ In America, dress according to the state in which you are and your industry.

✓ When in Germany, keep it classic and conservative.

✓ In Japan, stick to well-tailored suits and dresses.

✓ If you are a senior manager in the UAE, better wear a tie to work.

✓ In France, feel free to experiment with fashion while keeping it appropriate for the workplace.

✓ In the UK, maintain a balance by being not too conservative, but still keeping it formal.

MANAGING YOUR IMAGE: CONVERSATIONS WITH LEADERS

DR A. VELUMANI

Dr A. Velumani is the creator and Chief Executive Officer of Thyrocare, a brand worth over ₹2000 crores. He was born in a small village in Coimbatore to a landless farmer. He studied to be a mathematician and acquired his PhD in Thyroid Biochemistry from BARC. He worked in BARC for fourteen years as a research scientist and teacher before starting his own business.

Do you think it is important for people to present themselves correctly?

We are made of flesh and blood but when I talk to you I talk about who you are. So, I think dressing is important for people. What you wear reveals your personality. There are various kinds of bodies, and one should wear clothes that are not distracting.

Different jobs and places have diverse needs. But when it comes to corporate places, the continuity with which you present yourself, according to me, makes sense. For several reasons, I choose to wear black and white. I have been in business for twenty-five years. For the first ten years, I wore multiple colours, but later decided to go with black and white as it suits me the best. There are other CEOs who like to change their look every day and create suspense about their dressing.

Do you think it has worked in your favour to be consistent?

I like to believe that it worked because my mind is consistent, simple and frugal. I don't believe in spending more than ₹1499 for an outfit. I think pricier things looks vulgar. To a certain extent, a person who has less relevance to you on a day-to-day basis, would not mind seeing how he or she is dressed. When it comes to office, it is important for you to have consistency as well as uncompromised, fully acceptable dress code. I believe in practising formality.

Should CEOs wear T-shirts and look funky like the modern IT generation does?

Looking at people like Mark Zuckerberg, who have become billionaires before the age of thirty, all the people in the modern generation want to become billionaires before thirty. The other thing is that they have been school dropouts and it is foolish to copy them. I think we should learn from better people like Narayana Murthy. I do not insist that people who work for me should take up formal dressing. Sometimes they go off limits, but my office just developed a dress code for employees.

The guys who are wearing according to the dress code are said to be better off than the others. Even if you consider me, I wear suits when I come out. I consider the crowd, so that the person listening can understand that they are talking to someone big. Nowadays, I mix them with Modi coats.

Once I wear this, my face looks bright. When I wear just the shirt, the face looks darker. This I have observed in different interviews. So, it is physics that colour contrasting improves the detailed graph of dressing.

Do you think people form an impression when they meet others?

They do form an impression when meeting other people. Man is stupid enough to come to a decision about others within minutes or hours of meeting them. It so happens, in interviews, that someone is highly impressive but are ordinary in appearance. In my office, there are some people who are different from how they look. So, it is true that people form impressions very quickly. But the sooner they form an impression, the more wrong could be their idea.

Forming an opinion before getting a complete idea about the person is stupidity. People form an opinion based on hair and dress. People also form opinions on the length of the nose, smile, teeth, or even pimples. So, I am of the opinion that forming an impression fast is really bad.

If I need to work as an employee or employer for a long period of time, I think forming an opinion should take time. It could be wrong in both ways because there are people who come in for interviews wearing a suit but cannot speak English. So, if you are open and do not judge, you tend to be right.

Even when I was about to fire some people from the company, one of the managers came to me and said that those people are good at something and that we should keep them. Till now they are some of the best employees in the company. The only reason managers chose them was because they could not speak English. So, one must check for the true personality and not the displayed one. People should know from your dress that you are not too poor or too rich. You should wear decent clothes and have neatly combed hair.

Do you think it is important for people to stand by their value systems by how they present themselves?

1. First and foremost, if you change your personality for others' acceptance, you are stupid. Hence, your personality should be what you are. If you enjoy it, stick to it or if you do not enjoy it, change it. But do not go by what others think about you.

2. Everyone has a personality, be it good or bad. But, here, the question is not about that. It is about communication. Then there are three kinds of personalities:

   a. You have a good personality, but you do not know how to display. Until you communicate, I would not know about you.

   b. You have a bad personality, so you did not display.

   c. You have a bad personality but still, you present yourself intelligently.

   The challenge happens when good people cannot present themselves. That is an unfortunate situation and thus the importance of communication. So, a well-dressed man cannot become a leader but a fully communicating man can. You need to be able to express yourself.

What are your views on the frivolous attitude of business owners?

It is very important to communicate who you are as a person by your way of living. Every person has to adopt that kind of dressing to say it, do it and listen. People would know you for what you are, so if you are predictable, people around you would understand you.

What are your tips or guidelines for upcoming entrepreneurs on how to present themselves and become successful?

There is a single word – frugality. Don't spend on an outfit thinking that the neighbours or subordinates would appreciate it. When I was young, I wore similar shirts every time. So, for the youth, I would say be frugal, don't focus on impressing. The other thing is to be simple and don't distract. CEOs flaunt many brands because they tend to show off. They think it gets them an advantage, but it is not true.

*

SATYAKAM ARYA

Satyakam Arya started his career in the automotive industry with Maruti Suzuki. After one year of training, he moved to supply and management. After his stint at Maruti, he worked across various functions in various industries. He worked with an Italian company, then with Renault Nissan and then at Mahindra. For the past eight years, he has been working in the commercial vehicle industry.

What are your views on how important the first impression is in business?

For me, first impressions hold two main component – hygiene and entry strategy.

Ingredients required for a good entry strategy are:

- Dressing sense.
- How you carry yourself.
- How you start the conversation or how confident you are while making an entrance. To make a good entry strategy you should develop skills like your attitude, your behaviour and the stability of your mind.

Any specific incident you remember where you judged someone or you were judged by someone?

I interview a lot of people where the first impression is very important. This is the thing which is missing in a lot of people as it is not taught in academics, or in the professional life.

Do you believe that impressions are made in three to thirty seconds?

Unknowingly, we all form the first impression of others. For me, the first impression is the entry point. It's the first door to success and after that also you have to maintain your impression.

How important is personal branding in the corporate world?

It's very important, especially in India. India has changed dramatically in the last fifty years in terms of the business world. Fifty years ago, employees would dressed traditionally but now even the lowest level employee is confronted with globalization.

The transition took place quickly and without any support and guidance. So, academics and professionals don't teach such things in the curriculum. People learn through their own experiences.

Do you think that the dressing concept is superficial, and content is more important?

I feel content is very much important, but dressing is equally important, and companies should focus on this. It's important to dress according to the situation.

Do you think culture plays an important role in the way we present ourselves?

I think it plays an important role because it helps to build an impactful environment.

Do you think organizational philosophy about the way they present themselves is also impacting the employees' dressing sense?
Mahindra takes a lot of effort in being brand conscious and preparing people to get associated with the brand and how to present themselves.

How does the way people present themselves impact the organization?
If you want to attract the younger generation you should have to change traditional dressing style and traditional culture in the company because they don't accept this style. Non-traditional style brings informality in the culture and informal conversations generate new ideas. Many start-ups have informality in their behaviour.

Do you think personal branding is important for promotions?
If you have other qualities and don't dress properly, then you won't get selected.

How is personal branding important and does it differ from country to country in terms of acceptance?
In Europe, personal branding is quite known.

In the last fifteen years, I found that candidates from eastern and western countries give very different answers for the same question.

When you ask people in the West, 'Tell us something about yourself', the Westerner tells a short picture of his life, parents and previous job.

But in the East, the answer starts with what their job is, and each and every detail of the job. The interviewer gets bored with such details.

What is the difference between countries in implementing the things which they are already aware of?

In Europe and Japan, people are well dressed and know how to dress according to the occasion.

In India, I don't get this picture clearly. People tend to take it lightly.

When Indians work outside India would their dressing matter as they represent the corporate world and Brand India too?

If you don't know how to dress, then you wouldn't be here. The person who doesn't know this spoils their business relations.

What is your advice to upcoming people in the corporate world who want to succeed in life?

- Be sensitive.
- Work on the thing you don't know.
- Maintain standards.

*

AMBRAISH DASGUPTA

Ambraish Dasgupta is an electrical engineer. For the majority of his career, he has been in consulting. He started his career in technology brand and then gradually moved up to become a partner in 1987, and to become a consulting leader in 2007–2008.

Ambraish joined KPMG as a consulting leader. He has also been the chairman of Bengal commission of commerce and the chairman of commerce commission. Currently, he is working in the State Planning Board, and is an honorary committee member of the state strategic board.

Do you think we form an impression about people in the first meeting with them?

At a younger age, we form impressions very quickly about a person in the first meeting itself. But as we grow older, that starts to change, and we don't form impressions as quickly. When we meet the person more often, we try to form an opinion which is more informed and might be different from the previous one.

It also depends on the context of the meeting place. If we are meeting a person at a conference or a board meeting, we form a different opinion than when we meet the person if he came to give an interview.

A talented person may not belong to a wealthy family. So, we can see that we can't judge a person by the first meeting.

What factors do we look for when we form an impression about a person?

We see that respect always remains at the top of the list for any behavioural requirement. Our dressing must show respect to the other person.

A person might not belong to a wealthy family and hence can't afford branded clothes, but his clothes must be respectful towards the person he meets.

Casual clothes show less respect towards the person we are meeting. So, there should be an appropriate dressing sense.

Have you ever come across a person who was not showing respect to you or the situation by not wearing appropriate clothes?

Yes, many times. Some people think that they must present themselves as they are. They don't care about what others might think of them.

With this type of thinking, they unintentionally disrespect others by their inappropriate dressing.

Do you think culture plays a role when people are trying to project themselves differently?

If we go by the traditional culture of India, it's varied as it differs from south to north and east to west.

But the younger generation is going away from the traditional culture and hence creating their own culture.

When we work in corporate, we need to follow the culture of the organization and the industry.

Respect the occasion and people present at that occasion by dressing appropriately according to the occasion. By this, culture is also retained.

If I do not have proper dress for a particular occasion, then I shouldn't be there. Also, there must be respect towards comfort.

Who has inspired you in your dressing style in which you present yourself to the outside world?
Observation, point of view and also respect towards any occasion are factors which have inspired me a lot in my dressing sense.

How important is it to brand yourself with your values and what you stand for today?
It is very important. People judge you based on your power price, local price and corporate price. So today what you need is branding.

How important is to present yourself and your value systems?
It is extremely essential. If we try to sell a product, then the presentation of the product matters a lot more as compared to personal presentation.

I remember a funny story. Once I forgot to wear socks. I was delivering a presentation at a meeting and I was trying to cover it up with my trousers, but one of my colleagues noticed it and asked if I had forgotten to wear socks. That was really funny and embarrassing for me.

What is your recommendation to an upcoming consultant on how they represent themselves in terms of power dressing?
Respect the occasion, respect the people, present yourself right and act accordingly.

*

SAMEER SINHA

Sameer Sinha is a military veteran. He is now a speaker, thought leader, a teacher and a man who's out to inspire people to inspire themselves and others. Emerging from the triumphs and tragedies of war with a crystallized understanding of leadership in the most challenging environments, Sameer has put his knowledge to use in the business world.

Sameer presently heads the Human Resources department of Renault Nissan India. He offers solutions in leadership, strategy, innovation, management, team building, contingency planning and crisis management.

What's your experience with the people you interact with when you travel to different geographical places?
I have a wonderful experience being a soldier first, and then as an engineer, HR and a lot more. The journey has been long. A huge amount of learning came through this long journey. The one thing I liked the most about the Renault engineers is what they call themselves. Not engineers or architects but designers. They have a totally different approach in designing when compared to other designers.

I must say that the army has taught me a lot – the best lessons of my life. Today also I implement them in my work. I have developed a community feeling, and many such things are possible because of my army teachings.

What contributes to the community feeling, people going out of duty ?

Once you start thinking from a person's perspective then it becomes easy to develop such feelings. Renault takes care of the person and helps you settle down accordingly, which is the best thing about it.

The initial few days in an organization decide how long a person will stay in the organization.

What's your opinion about the first impression and how does it make a difference when it comes to people and their brand?

To my mind, the first impression is when we get connected to the person while talking to him/her and generate an opinion about the person. It results in determining the way we behave with the person.

The first impression gives an idea of what you stand for.

What percentage does the first impression contribute in decision making?

Three aspects relate here for how the first impression affects decision making:
- How you present yourself and your physical appearance.
- Confidence that one exudes towards the other.
- Intelligence.

To what extent do you think the first impression is accurate?

I won't say that. But definitely, they give us some impression.

Decisions are made based on opinions. If we think that the person is good then we continue with the interview for long, and if not, then we just talk a little bit and say 'nice to have you here'. The first impression decides our opinion about a person.

Have you ever met someone who was not appropriately dressed or not presentable?
Just yesterday I was talking to a candidate and I asked him about his future goals. He was planning to move from France to Italy but was not clear on what he wanted to do. This makes him unpresentable.

Who has inspired your dressing style?
I think the army has taught me a lot. First thing the army teaches you is confidence. The second thing it taught me is to be at the right place at the right time in proper uniform.

Being appropriately dressed with the right etiquette is the most important lesson learnt from my army background. In schools, dressing properly was the most important part in the olden times. Now, it's not that strict as it once was. Now students are also moulding themselves according to the environment.

What according to you is personal branding?
- Physical appearance and how you dress up.
- How presentable you are, the smile you give to others, the handshake you give, all of it makes a difference.
- Confidence.

Do you think personal value can be depicted in the way a person dresses or appears?
Yes, I think so, up to an extent.

How are cultures and brands different across different geographies, across India and in other countries?
I think all the three aspects mentioned earlier are actually creating a difference in India and in other countries.

We must be sensitive towards each and every culture. Our values are driven by family so it's different at different places.

How is personal branding important in the HR field?
It is very important. I interact with lots of people in their interviews. I focus on how they present themselves. It's important to understand the people behind the clothes.

I want to share an example here. A few days ago, I interviewed a person and asked him one question – what colour shoes do army people wear? He could easily guess that by seeing our shoes, which were clearly visible to him. But he said he was not sure and the reason he gave was that he came from a poor background and couldn't afford shoes. But we also saw sweat on his forehead, which indicated that he had got stuck on that question. When the results were announced, and he was rejected, he asked me if he was rejected because he was wearing sandals. I said yes but the reason was not actually this, it was something else. So how you present yourself to others is different from how the person sees you.

What role does organizational culture play when it comes to presenting yourself?

We take a lot of pride in asking others how much time they take to get ready in the morning because we all get ready in just a few minutes. We just have to put on a shirt with the Renault logo on it and we are ready. Due to the uniformity in the system, we connect with the people more.

*

YASH VASANT

Yash Vasant has a degree in Neuroscience and Economics from Los Angeles. Having successfully started and handled eight different businesses, he is today recognized as one of the youngest and leading speakers of India. He has helped  and groomed over 5000 business and social leaders in India.

Yash is the founder of BNI in Ahmedabad and was recently recognized as the world's youngest Executive Director of BNI. With over twenty International Awards under his belt, he aspires to bring about a change in his great country by influencing the influencers.

Do you think people form impressions randomly about other individuals?

Yes, everyone forms an impression. I studied neuroscience and I specialize in behavioural psychology. I look at people from different aspects.

For me, one's dressing style matters a lot. I can guess whether the person's mind is subconscious or conscious at that moment. The expression expresses a lot about the present state of mind.

Have you ever encountered any situation where you were not properly dressed?

I can't remember such a situation as it has never happened in the recent past. It's a part of my identity that I am always well dressed.

I remember one situation where I was dressed according to the occasion but still felt a little embarrassed. It was at a Halloween party. I dressed up as Superman, with the red underwear. No one else was dressed to that extent in the whole party and that was embarrassing.

As an interviewer do you observe the dressing style of the candidates?
Yes, I do care about it because having an idea is not enough. How you execute that idea matters a lot. If you are not able to take care of your dressing style then how can I rely on you to handle my company? I expect the candidates coming for the interview to be well groomed.

Do you think culture plays an important role in the way you present yourself?
Surely it plays an important role. I believe that one's dressing style gets inspired from the culture you belong to and reflects that culture truly.

What is your personal style of dressing?
Mine is a classic look. My style is simple and elegant.

Can you give me the names which come to your mind when it comes to power dressing?
I would say James Bond and Shah Rukh Khan. I like to dress like a person I want to be. Always dress for tomorrow. I live the lifestyle of a billionaire, but I am not a billionaire.

What impact does power dressing have on interactions with people?

If you are wearing a shirt and trousers and if your shirt is not tucked in properly or you have not worn a tie or your shoes are not polished, then these things will affect your personality and you won't get proper respect from the other person.

Does Western or Eastern dressing affect one's dressing style?

I think men wearing properly ironed dhoti and kurta would be power dressing in terms of a village. There he won't have to wear a suit to get power dressed. It does not matter whether you dress in Western or Eastern clothes, what is important is to be dressed properly.

What is your advice to upcoming entrepreneurs on power dressing?

Be comfortable in what you wear.

Dress according to the occasion. Emulate the person you are going to meet.

Don't try to save a penny on the way you look because those pennies might cost you your future.

*

JOGENDRA SINGH

Jogendra Singh is an accomplished finance professional. He was the first employee of Daimler India Commercial Vehicles. Apart from articulating finance, he stands out with his adroit skills of dealing with people, empowering his teams and creating leaders.

Jogendra enjoys imparting his experience and knowledge to the younger generation and interacts with the students of many professional institutes. He showcases optimism in each approach of his professional as well as personal life.

What have you done in the last few years of your service in your company?

It has been very interesting. Last year, in December, we organized India's largest art exhibition which consisted of multicultural and multifaceted art. We put drama and circus in the same campus. The idea was to revive circus art through the medium of drama. It was held in Goa over eight days at different locations with fifty-four projects.

Prior to that, I was with Daimler as I was a member of the initial team that set up the plant. I am really happy that I have converted that green field into such a big factory.

How long have you been in the finance industry? What is your background in finance?

I have spent three decades in finance. The journey has been fruitful. At that time, when I passed chartered accountancy in 1987, it was thought that CAs are dry people. I used to say that I am me, CA is just a part of my personality.

How do you stand out from the group of regular chartered accountants?

In the finance field, content is very important. My office does not just have books on chartered accountancy, but also books on poetry, women personalities and so on. By facilitating different areas, one can develop himself/herself. Also singing and dancing brings us closer to the real world. Communicating with new people is also a good habit that helps to develop personality.

In a way, you are always selling yourself through your words, action and pitch. You could sell any product, dream, the vision of a leader, an excuse, explanation or argument. You are always selling yourself for a situation. For this, you have to be ready mentally, understand the topic and content very well.

You complement it with other parts of your life – the way you speak, the way you express yourself, your dress, the way you create a network with people, and the way you interact with people.

A person is the sum total of the different parts of his life.

You have to prepare yourself to be what you are and the need to put yourself in a package. You have to say you are unique. Uniqueness is important because sameness sucks.

You have to position yourself, that is, you have to cover yourself in different ways like:

1. Your smile.
2. Your way of interaction with people.
3. The way you dress.

Do you see that the way you present yourself externally affects how people perceive you?

Absolutely. This happens not only in India but in other countries too.

One thing is important when you meet people; you have only one chance to create that first impression. So, your dressing style must be appropriate and according to the occasion.

What are the aspects that go into personal presence?

When I look at a person, the first thing I see is the kind of energy he is producing. Whether I am receiving the right or wrong energy. It's important to send your positivity to others and to convert it into your impression.

There should be other traits as well, like one's biggest ornament is the smile. The second thing is your dressing style. The third is to be a good listener. You have to understand the need of the person sitting across the table. Only then will you be able to deliver what he/she wants. You have to compliment yourself with all these things to create your presence.

Have you ever met a person who is not appropriately dressed?
It has happened many times. We come across many people who are inappropriately dressed for the occasion.

Over the last few years, casual dressing has crept into the business world. Also, we are seeing many new entrepreneurs who require investors to invest in their start-ups. As an investor, I have observed many people new in business. When they come to us, they are appropriately dressed. Dressing according to the occasion is very important in my opinion.

Is there anyone who has inspired your dressing style?
You should have your own sense on how to dress according to the occasion. You should be able to select the stuff that suits your personality. You can't imitate others as people have different personalities.

You only get inspiration from others but it's your choice how to dress. Make sure that you are comfortable in what you are wearing.

Sunil Mujal, our chairman, has inspired me a lot in terms of dressing. He dresses smartly. Your style must reflect your attentiveness.

How important is personal branding in the corporate world today?
I think everyone is a brand for himself/herself. The thing that matters is how you present yourself in front of others. Your style and how you deliver your content matters a lot.

Skills and talent with inappropriate dressing sense are useless. In my view, brand is a reputation. It is important to create your reputation. It takes a long time to develop and requires a conscious effort. Maintaining it is very important, more than developing it.

Is the first impression important?
Yes, it matters. Many a time we see that people with the same skill, talent and logic get their first break at different points of time.

To create your own impression, you have to distinguish yourself from others. In one way or another, I believe first impressions last for long.

Let me share my personal experience here. I received this job offer from Mr Sunil Mujal. He was impressed by my dressing style and called me for the interview. So, this proves that first impressions are extremely important.

What do you think of the younger generation that is coming into this corporate world?
In schools and colleges, personal branding is not that important. The personality traits that one should have are honesty, goodness and other values.

If you are a billionaire and you go around in casuals, nobody will ask you a single question. It doesn't matter anymore because of your success and fame. You may dress as you wish.

What is your advice to our readers?

- Opportunities in today's world are limitless. So don't dream small, dream big. Without this attitude, you can't achieve anything.
- Prepare yourself to pursue your dream.
- Reputation takes a long time to build. Take care of it.
- Always stay healthy and live life to the fullest.

*

RAJIV TALREJA

Rajiv Talreja is a serial entrepreneur and a business coach for over a decade and is known for the exponential growth he has created for his clients. He currently runs three successful businesses – Quantum Leap Learning  Solutions, DreamCraft Events and Entertainment and DreamCatcher Investments.

He has had two business failures in the past which he believes have been his best experiences. Over the last decade, Rajiv has impacted over 50,000 people through his Training and Coaching Engagements across 150+ corporate organizations and over 5000 business owners.

What are your views on creating a first impression?
I believe human beings are judging machines which constantly judge every individual's acts.

I always say that a book is always judged by its cover. No one will pick up a book that has a boring cover.

We always say that the Earth is a beautiful planet and we are the ones who make it beautiful. Therefore, every individual is judged on the way one is dressed and presents himself/herself in public. Looks are not in our control but how we carry ourselves is important.

When it comes to the first impression, it's all about the ease and comfort with which you carry yourself.

What goes into the ease and comfort of carrying yourself?
Here I want to share an example of my friend who is in Germany and is a plastic surgeon. She always says that most patients are unhappy after plastic surgery, even if their looks are better than before. The fundamental reason behind this is that they are not internally accepting of the change in themselves.

So, it's all about your internal acceptance which makes you carry yourself with ease and comfort.

A few things which go into this are:

- Acceptance of yourself. Are you happy with who you are?
- Appropriateness in the way you carry yourself, your hairstyle, your grooming, your looks.

How difficult is it for Mark Zuckerberg to make his way?
The world is an unfair place and generally gives you permission to be how you want to be on the basis of your bank balance. Mark Zuckerberg has created that permission for himself to do what he wants from his genius and bank balance.

I would say that those who can make it big can exercise the right to carry themselves however they want. But till that point, you have to follow some norms of society. When we talk about power dressing, it also follows certain rules but if we are not comfortable then there is no need for such dressing. But people follow the rule book of power dressing to look good and ignore comfort.

Is there any incident that you remember when you judged someone by his/her bad appearance but later realized that this is not the case?

I would like to share my personal experience here. I have been in training and coaching business for the last ten years. I started at the age of twenty. I am vertically challenged. I am 5 feet and 5 inches tall. I was always judged negatively when I visited a programme. I was given suits to wear to look mature. But during that time, suits didn't suit me.

In my case, first impressions didn't work. They rejected my book without even looking at it once. They discarded me because of my personal appearance. I find the cover of the book to be critical. Even if your product and services are great, if you don't market it, then nobody will buy your product.

Do you think the culture of a place plays an important role when you are a speaker within or outside the country?

During my initial years, when I went to corporate places to do my training programmes, they wouldn't judge me based on my clothes. If I wore formal trousers with shirts, they would accept me as a trainer. On the other hand, an industrialist would seek a person wearing a tie and suit for the trainer's job.

This is only due to the diversity in culture. My friend working in Chicago would be accepted in casuals. So, it is different for different places.

Does your attire change according to geographical boundaries?
I don't change my attire based on geographical boundaries. As a speaker, I have definitely thought through my personal branding in terms of what attire I would wear when I visit any geographical place.

For meetings with officials, I need to keep suits as I have to maintain standards. Also, I need to keep casuals and some sort of traditional outfit from that geographical location.

More the familiarity with the person increases, more casual my dressing becomes with them.

Do you think personal branding plays an important role in the industry?
It reminds people of you in future. It is like a recall. I want to share an experience. For my three-day trip to the south, I decided to wear bandis and carried eight or nine different coloured ones. On the very first day, I wore a bandi with rolled up full-sleeved shirt. I got many compliments for the outfit. I continued to wear the same kind of outfit just with different colours for the next two days. On the third day, I saw two men wearing a bandi and shirt combination that was similar to my style. I realized that my style had become a brand.

Who has inspired you in the way you dress?
My wife is my inspiration. I am lucky that I got married to a very pretty girl. She taught me how to carry my clothes. In my college days, I used to wear formal trousers with the shirt

tucked out and sleeves folded. I never bothered about my dressing. She made me realize that I am a brand and people judge you by your dressing style.

But I give all credit to my college. I rebelled at that time against wearing a tie. Even now I don't wear a tie. I believe that a tie ties you down. Comfort is my number one priority when I am dressing.

Can our clothes depict the personal values that we have?

Absolutely yes. I believe that our clothes are a reflection of our personal values. My value is to be easy, comfortable, to be grounded and real as a person.

Do you think people are aware of the concept of personal branding?

Very few people understand this. Many entrepreneurs lose their confidence because they are wearing something very uncomfortable. For me, power dressing is the sense of dressing in which you feel comfortable. In BNI, there was a sculptor whose kurtas with formal pants had become his trademark. Suddenly, he was given the position of a Director Consultant and was forced by the company to wear suits. But I knew that he was more comfortable in those kurtas and not in these suits.

Do you teach personal branding concepts in your training programme?

I don't teach them because I am not an expert. But if somebody comes to me and they want my suggestions, I surely give them.

What differences do you see in the corporate world when we talk about personal branding and power dressing?

The funny part is that when you walk into a corporate world you assume that you will meet people wearing only formals there. We have created that kind of mentality. I think there is a need for education on dressing, especially in the IT sector. A lot of times I have seen these guys mismatching their dress and accessories. There is a lot of confusion about the appropriate dressing sense. It is a lack of awareness and educational issue. What you wear has to be appropriate and match the occasion.

What is your recommendation for upcoming business entrepreneurs?

Rule of comfort with appropriateness must be followed. Do something in your dressing that leaves a memory of you on others. Stand out, be different from others.

*

BIJU CHANDRAN

Biju Chandran is a practising chartered accountant specializing in creation management of NGOs. He was committee member of GMCS course in southern India Regional Council of the Institute of Chartered Accountants of India for 2015-2016.

Currently, Biju is the President of the International Chamber of Indirect Tax Professionals – an organization created to impart knowledge on indirect taxes. He is also the Executive Director of Business Network International (BNI) Chennai CBD, a region which was ranked among the top ten regions in the world in the year 2016.

You have performed many roles – have you ever seen people forming impressions about each other?
Of course. When you are invited to a forum, people observe you closely. When you walk into the room they observe your dress, the way you talk, and thereby create a perception of you, or as we call it 'the first impression'.

Does this impression affect one's opinion about others?
I think we subconsciously form an opinion about a person by just seeing his behaviour and looks in the first six seconds of meeting them. Our whole conversation with them depends on that opinion which we have already taken in the first few seconds.

What aspects go into creating a first impression, apart from clothes?

The way they walk in, their postures, their shoulder position, eye contact, communication skills are all such things that I look for before creating an impression about others.

Any specific incident where you judged an individual and formed an impression of him/her?

Several times when you walk into big meetings, there is always one guy who stands out in the crowd. You want to know about him, and your eagerness to know him causes you to make favourable perceptions about him. You might think that the guy is a celebrity, or very reputed. Whenever we meet a big personality, this generally happens.

Any specific incident where you judged someone at the first meeting, but your judgement was not accurate?

Yes. In chartered accountancy (CA), there are many people who are technically very strong. People look up to them. We have heard a lot about such a person but have not met them personally. We create an image of this person that is high profile, very well-dressed, etc.

But when we meet them personally, we realize that their dressing sense is basic and our comprehension of this person is totally inaccurate. This happens a lot in my profession.

In traditional companies, your technical skills matter more than outward show in the CA field.

But when you work with MNCs, the way you present yourself matters a lot. If you have to meet corporate executives, they have some expectations from you.

Any personal experience where you were not appropriately dressed; how did you feel and how did others behave with you?
I have a standard set of coats and sleeveless jackets. People always say that this is Chandran's style. But there are occasions where I don't wear these. So, then people come and ask me what has happened to my signature style.

Sometimes when I wear T-shirt and jeans at some social functions, they come up and tell me that this is the first time they have seen me in casuals.

Do you think culture plays a role in the way you dress?
In BNI, our founder always says that culture precedes strategy. Culture is a primary ingredient in any organization. Culture is definitely very important when you want to groom yourself.

You have your own signature style. Is there anyone special who has inspired your style?
I can say that Amitabh Bachchan has a great personality. He keeps upgrading his style. Whatever he wears becomes a benchmark. All the accessories he wears start trending immediately. I admire him a lot for his dressing style.

Do you think you can present your value system? Can personal branding be based on the clothes you wear?

If you only wear one particular style, then it itself becomes a brand. Today, most people know me because of my style of coats. It definitely creates the branding of a person.

The way you talk, voice modulation, body language, respect for others, etc., are the other aspects one should focus on for personal branding. Also, the language we use creates a significant impact on people. So, it should be focused on more.

As a CA you can't market and advertise yourself. How important does branding become for you when you have to present yourself to the world?

We have to communicate with the client without any advertisement. The way we present our paper, the way we talk to officials and our behaviour with clients are the things that matter a lot. These things create an image of me for the others. Next time, when I meet them, my first impression ensures that they will be friendly within just a few minutes of communication.

What is your personal style? Are you conscious about what you are going to wear to work when you wake up?

Yes, when I wake up, I plan the whole day and decide my clothes accordingly. I always carry an extra shirt with me for unplanned occasions and also a gym outfit which I require in the morning itself.

Do you think that in business forums people are conscious about clothes? What they are wearing today?

Partially, yes, but predominantly, no. In our profession, preference is given to the skills, and not the looks. Society has already created an image of a CA in their mind and they judge us on our skills.

What are your recommendations for upcoming professionals in CA?

For our upcoming students, I would just like to say that they should focus on their communication skills. Every time you will meet a new client who will be different from the previous one. They all have to be handled differently and, hence, you should be able to communicate with them properly. Also, you must keep in mind your dressing style. The person you are going to meet is a respectful person in society, so you should not disrespect him by the way you are dressed. There are plenty of tips available on the Internet. They should search for it and start inculcating good practices in life. In the beginning, it will be difficult, but in a few years, it will become a part of your life. Then, you will be effortlessly doing these things.

*

MARION GILLICH

Marion Gillich was born in Romania and grew up in Germany. She is thirty-six years old and married to an Indian. She has lived in India for the past seven years. She encourages gender fairness.

Currently, Marion is heading the dealer network and sales governance department at Daimler India Commercial Vehicles Pvt. Ltd. She is planning to shift to New Rome as the Vice President of Marketing and Sales of Africa and Asia/Pacific at the automotive financial company.

Do you believe in first impressions when you meet people?
Yes, I think first impressions are important, especially in the corporate environment. When we interact with the dealer, we meet him once or twice. So, there first impressions are very important. Your body language, the way you walk, the way you speak, your behaviour and, most importantly, the way you are dressed are crucial factors which develop the first impressions of the person.

How do these impressions impact others' decision?
When we create an impression about a person we don't just notice his knowledge but also the external appearance. If you have great knowledge but do not have good dressing style, then your external appearance will not reflect your knowledge.

Your clothes reflect a lot about your personality. So, how you are dressed is the most important thing.

Have you ever had an experience when you were not properly dressed and how did you feel?
I remember a situation where I was dressed properly but feeling uncomfortable in it. I might have worn a shirt or a blouse showing a little more cleavage than usual, but it was still decent. A man in a meeting was paying more attention to my cleavage than my face. I was really very uncomfortable. In such situations, women generally blame themselves for making such mistakes, but the fault is of the man who was paying attention to the wrong place.

When you feel uncomfortable, you get distracted from your work. When you see a man looking where he shouldn't be, you feel disrespected and lose confidence.

Self-confidence is related to how people look at you. This incident took place in India, but the man was not Indian.

What role does culture play when such incidents take place?
I think culture plays an important role. In the example mentioned earlier, if the man was Indian, then he would not be looking at me so bluntly. He might have ignored me completely.

Also, if we talk about gender, a woman is not greeted in the same way as the man in the corporate world.

In terms of your dressing, Indians and Germans don't bother about what you wear but they bother about your behaviour. In the US, they are dressed casually. But in other places, dressing is a status symbol.

As you travel a lot, do you think culture plays an important role when you talk about north India and south India, not only professionally but also in other ways?
Yes, there is a little difference. In India, I have travelled to almost every state. In the south, they are taken aback. They are conservative and women are ignored, but in the north, they are more interactive and try to come into your personal space.

I think people are not aware about the concept of personal space. The reason, I think, maybe that there are a lot of people in India and you can't actually respect everybody's personal space. If you enter a bus or a train, you have to break someone's personal space to move forward due to the lack of luxury to keep the personal space. But they just don't understand that in the office you have the luxury to keep within your personal space. They are not aware of it. They have to be told.

How important is it for leaders to have the right image when they project themselves globally?
I think it's becoming more and more important. The perception becomes a reality. It is really important for political as well as industrial leaders to maintain the right image, to maintain their credibility. This is because what they preach is not reflected by their external appearance.

Since you moved to India, how has it been different from your male counterparts?

When I first moved to India, I was not engaged. I was single. I told people that I am engaged just to keep my image. At that time, I was in my early thirties. In India, it is thought that a woman who is not engaged till the thirties might have some problem. But if there was a man in the same position as me, he may not face this issue.

Also, there were only a few women where I worked. There I might have been dressed differently from others and I might have behaved differently.

Do you think that now corporates are moving towards a gender-neutral environment? If yes, then how?

I think somewhere it has happened, but there is still a long way to go. Again, if we talk about gender fairness, there is no fairness at all in the corporate world. People are conditioned to see men as more competent than women. Due to this, women require quota – not to show that they are more powerful than men, but to play on the same field as them. I think it will take a couple of years for this to change.

Do you think stereotype is a subconscious thought and applies to all women, and how far are women responsible for it?

I have daily encounters with stereotypes and some of them are very much real. In India, two days back, I was talking to my manager and we were discussing a vacancy in the audit team. We were looking for an auditor who would have to travel a lot. I suggested a girl's name who was qualified for this post. But my manager said that she was married and would not be allowed to travel. She was actually not allowed to travel, when I asked her about it. I think these kinds of stereotypes are true to a certain extent because of the inhibitions that exist in women's mindsets. We not only need to break stereotypes in men's minds, but in women's minds as well.

How are the East and the West different in such cases?

It is more or less the same in western countries as well. But in the West, it might not be to that extent because of the acceptance of a working woman by the family.

In Germany, there was actually a law that allowed women to be paid more if she stayed at home. So, we see that politics also supports gender inequality.

Can you share some incidents where you experienced gender insensitivity?

A couple of weeks ago, I was supposed to take an assessment level task as an assessor. Assessment level is the first level to cross to become a manager. A man entered the room and greeted us by saying, 'Good morning, gentlemen'. I was shocked, but didn't say anything. When he was leaving, he again said, 'Thank you, gentlemen'. I was really shocked.

Among the three assessors, I was completely ignored by him.

When I gave him the results and told him about his mistake, he was very embarrassed and felt sorry. But he was not aware of it at all. This is not done intentionally but due to conditioning in their mindset.

How conducive is the corporate environment today in accepting women in senior manager positions?

I see good signs but we're not there yet. If you look at stats, about 51 per cent of global inhabitants are females. But in the corporate world, only 6.5 per cent CEOs are women. It is a long way to go. For this reason, we have to bring in the quota system to break this kind of thinking

Do men give respect to women when they actually deserve it for their knowledge, ability and skills or does their gender overshadow their skills?

Most men, unfortunately, ignore women, as I already told you, with the assessment example. They are not aware of it and already have their mind set like this.

In Germany, in 1960s-70s, it was normal for a man to say that he needed a nice-looking secretary. We know that the sex hormones are responsible for attraction from the opposite sex. But it's our body and only we can control it. But men are not being told about it, so they are unaware of it.

What is your recommendation for a woman who wants to step up the ladder in the corporate world?

You have to be tough, and not get discouraged easily. You have to be stronger than men. Women sometimes have to collect all the self-resistance and confidence to fight their way through. Raise your voice if you are feeling uncomfortable about anything.

What is your dressing style?

I am very conscious about what I wear. My style of dressing is sporty, elegant and I love to wear high heels. I prefer to wear flats if I have to travel. We have to find the right balance between elegance and convenience.

I am really very inspired by Christine Lagarde (the Managing Director of the International Monetary Fund) when it comes to dressing and presenting yourself. She is a senior lady but her entire expression and the way she dresses is always proper. She dresses professionally.

What are your views when it comes to power dressing in corporate India.

For women, it's not fully understood because people are not aware of it. They generally wear salwar-kurtas and saree. I find the saree a very beautiful garment to wear. But the saree doesn't hide the belly and it takes away the attention of others from their work. I also think salwar-kurtas are very flowery and distracting.

Although you can wear casual clothes, they must be powerful. They must be ironed, shoes must be polished, and clothes must be free from stain.

What is your experience from rest of the world like Japan, Singapore or any other place?

It is normal to wear short skirts and clothes that show off your body. But I think they grab others' attention. It's not a powerful dressing style.

Other countries are more liberal in dressing than India but not equal to power dressing. Dress the way that underlines your professionalism.

What, according to you, is personal branding for an individual?

It is the combination of the way you dress, speak and behave. Apart from these, you have to be fit. If you respect your body and health, it will create an impression that you respect others too as you respect yourself.

As a leader, you should always try to be a role model. As a leader, you have to live up to the values that you preach to others. People might not give you the respect, but might give respect to the position.

Do you see a difference in the way Indian speakers and presenters present themselves from others?

Indians are a bit more personal. They bring a lot of examples from their personal life while presenting something, whereas others follow professionalism. They are more on the rational side than the emotional side.

What is your recommendation to young professionals on personal branding? What do they need to keep in mind?
They should think of what their values are. A lot of people just don't have values. If you want to shape something in the work environment you need values.

Key Takeaways:
- Personality of a person is reflected mostly by their dressing style.
- In the corporate environment, there is a need to encourage gender fairness.
- Personal branding is done by proper dressing.

*

SAURABH JAGGI

Saurabh Jaggi works as a director for a Swiss bank, based in Singapore. A multifaceted individual, he holds a Master's in Leading Innovation and Change from UK and has over twenty-two years of corporate experience, primarily driving Process Excellence (PEx) in financial services, besides extensive experience and passion for training/coaching people on Leadership and PEx. He is well travelled, very fond of dressing up and a self-certified food enthusiast.

What are your views on the first impression?

If I talk about the media and entertainment industry, we always keep a watch on looks. We notice each and every change in a person belonging to the big or small screen. We notice beards, attire, modulation in voice, language spoken by a person, the views of the person, the content the person wants to deliver. These are generally key points which create the first impression about a person. Somewhere you start liking or disliking the person based on this first impression.

There is a saying, 'First impression is the best and last impression'. I believe in it to an extent. I believe first impressions might not be your last impression, but surely it will last for a long period of time. It can't be changed easily. After creating an impression about a person in our mind, we interact with the person according to that impression.

Therefore, one has to be very careful while creating an impression on others.

Can you recall any incident where you were not appropriately dressed according to the place and how you felt then?

Let's take an example of the banking sector. If you are working in a unit then a well-dressed employee with a tie is called a smart employee.

If you dress in jeans and T-shirt, it will be a mismatch. If you are invited to a theme party and you are supposed to wear according to the prescribed dress code, but you wear something contrary to the dress code, then you are inappropriately dressed.

The factors on which our dressing should be decided are environment, place, event, people who invited us, etc. I want to share my experience here. When I was in first year, I was invited to a theme party where you were supposed to wear a black suit and a bow tie. But I reached the party in denims, shirt and denim jacket. When I stepped in, I felt really embarrassed. But I somehow handled the situation.

We all know that dress doesn't matter but the motive of the party matters. But at that time, I really felt embarrassed due to the many eyes looking at me.

How does culture play a role in shaping impressions of people?

The banking and financial services have many international companies in many cities of India and I do feel a difference here. And when we talk about culture, every industry has a culture of its own.

If we talk about an industry in Delhi, there people wear formals. But as we move to Mumbai, people dress in a more casual, smart style. In Bangalore and some other places, I see many people from the IT sector wearing sandals and slippers to the office. It really creates a bad impression, wearing slippers and sandals with trousers and coming to the office.

I had started my career with the hotel industry. There I had to look presentable all the time. It didn't matter whether you were tired or working on a holiday.

I think dressing sense develops from the environment we are working in, the atmosphere we studied in, and also our upbringing. All these things are really important for grooming a person.

Does your behaviour get reflected in the kind of clothes you wear?

If we take the example of Virat Kohli, he belonged to a middle-class family from Delhi. So, the kind of clothes need not depict the kind of person.

Generally, our dressing is based on environmental conditions and the people around us, and not on our behaviour.

But there is one thing that a person belonging to the middle class prefers; wearing a creased shirt instead of wearing an ironed shirt.

If I have to attend a meeting, I would be formally dressed, wearing a wrist watch and a tie. But walking on the streets in formals would make me look weird and therefore I need to wear casuals here.

What is your personal style of dressing?

Five days in a week I work as an officer. I usually have to travel internationally and extensively. For those five days, I dress completely in a formal attire with my shirt tucked in, with pocket squares and in polished shoes. On Sunday, I generally wear casuals like trousers and T-shirts. I also like to wear Modi jackets on some occasions which give an Indo-western look to my style.

Who has inspired your dressing style?

The person who created the first impression on me in terms of dressing was Mr Kundanlal Jaggi. He is a pioneer in the restaurant industry. He always wakes up at 5.30 a.m. and by 6.00 a.m., he is ready in a proper suit and Peshwari *pagdi* (turban). On special occasions, he wears Pathani and Achkans. He created a great impression on me.

Could you share some names from the Indian corporate world who are into power dressing?

The first person that comes to my mind is Mr Amitabh Bachchan. I am greatly impressed by his dressing style on any occasion.

Other celebrities who dress in jeans and shirt and look good are not actually power dressed according to me.

Mr Ratan Tata is another person who comes to my mind.

Also, the enthusiasm created by Prime Minister Narendra Modi for power dressing has impressed me a lot. He is a very good example of power dressing. Now the Nehru jacket is being called the Modi jacket and that is what we call personal branding.

Do you think power dressing is an Indian concept?
Actually, we are really far from power dressing. There is a lot more left to do. It's important for Indians to understand the importance of power dressing. It helps in creating a great impression on others. Some people are moving towards it.

What do you think goes into the personal branding of an individual?
It is a combination of three things. The way you look, the way you communicate (thinking, writing and speaking), and the way you act. This combination helps in creating personal branding of an individual.

What is your advice for people in India who want to compete in the corporate world?
All I have to say is based on my experience. If somebody wants to make it big in the corporate world, he/she always has to dress for success.

That would create a certain favourable impression on others and gradually lead to the branding of the individual. Although a person may not have interacted with you, the way you dress, the way you speak, the way you walk, all these create your impression on others.

Make sure you have positive thoughts, good mission, high goal in life and also good mentors in life. Keep moving forward. Remain grounded.

Be honest even in the most difficult situations. It will give you pain for some time, but eventually it will lead to your branding. I also think there is no replacement for hard work and preparation.

*

MURALI SUNDARAM

Murali Sundaram is an author, happyness coach, entrepreneur, keynote speaker and an acclaimed international trainer. For the last twenty years, he has been training, motivating and helping people stay happy and successful. He is an NLP trainer/therapist with NFNLP USA, a neuro feedback and bio feedback trainer and a psychological counsellor. He also specializes in neuroscience, yogic science, management science and pharmaceutical science. An ardent yoga practitioner, Murali is involved in teaching swara yoga, kriya yoga, gnana yoga and Reiki.

Murali has successfully trained more than 1,50,000 professionals, entrepreneurs, executives and students on personal, managerial and leadership effectiveness, organizational development, peak performance and wellness.

Below are excerpts from an interview between the author and Mr Murali Sundaram (MS):

Author: I have attended several meetings at BNI and have always seen 'appearance' to be a critical component to everyone who represents the organization at both regional and national levels. Is it a conscious effort taken by members at BNI to project themselves in a particular way?

MS: Every member at BNI is encouraged to believe themselves to be a leader. It is a business community and members look up to each other and follow what's true to their role and purpose of being in the organization. As leaders, we discuss the importance of corporate dressing and everyone knows that they have to come in level 3 or level 4 dressing to any formal BNI event. We do not prescribe this as a procedure rather practice it every time, so everyone follows it. This is how we manage the culture at BNI. Moreover, business attire becomes a must in business networking meetings as you can create a strong impression based on your attire. The executive leaders at BNI keep educating and inspiring our fellow members about the importance of dressing. Members also show keen interest and learn to dress well by listening to a lot of podcasts and online references. I am glad a book on such a topic is soon to be released by you.

Author: You are one of the very few leaders who talk a lot about the importance of dressing and impression through podcasts and lectures. Is there any specific reason for this?

MS: Yes, that's right. I personally believe that there is a very strong correlation between dressing, impression and personal branding, and it is extremely important to be conscious about it. Many sources are available to teach you what to do. However, very few that help you know how to do. Showing how to do is more powerful than saying how to do.

Author: You recently spoke about the personal branding of Sadhguru Jaggi Vasudev? Do you think personal branding plays a role in presenting yourself?

MS: In simple words, personal branding is all about your reputation. If you are an expert, entrepreneur, premiere or a professional, you rely on your skills and knowledge. Many of the competitors here would not argue about your skills and knowledge, whereas a customer always looks up to your brand value or your reputation first. So personal branding as a reputation is a must for everyone irrespective of their background and that's what make you wanted, famous or paid. Experts like Sadhguru Jaggi Vasudev have complemented their skills and knowledge with strong personal branding and reputation over a period of time. There may be another expert as knowledgeable as him, however, he would not be known to the world unless he has built a brand value and reputation for himself.

Author: What goes into developing personal branding? What should one do to create it?

MS: There are various elements that go into it and even small things count in the process. The way you dress, your body language, the way you adapt in an environment, the way you smile, the way you present yourself online and offline, how you interact with people, the way others perceive you based on your actions and commitments, and the list can continue. Creating a personal brand takes time but it is easy if it's got the commitment and determination of the one who believes in its power.

Author: There has been a growing count of people who claim themselves as trainers, mentors and coaches. Every second person in the community says so. How does personal branding become important for you and how do you try to distinguish yourself from others? Any recommendations?

MS: Very true! There are many trainers out there and probably many think that it's very easy to become a trainer if you have good communication skills and the ability to sharpen your skills by listening to or watching some learning resources. While there is nothing wrong about it, ultimately it is the niche that you create for yourself and the personal branding that would make you stand apart. You need to have a 'specialist area' and build your reputation and experience around it. Unless you have both, it is tough to sustain in today's world. A trainer can no longer take a 'generalist approach' without branding and reputation, and this holds true for any person in any profession. An expert trainer should be able to talk about his/her experiences from life, how he/she handled challenges and overcame various situations or what he/she has learnt from experience. The ability to influence the audience comes with experience. Personal values, success stories and failures become important to be understood and taught so people know how you have done for yourself first before you can teach others. To tell someone how to become successful, one has to talk from their real life experiences rather than reel life stories. These things only help improve personal branding and your reputation.

Author: You have been participating in workshops and forums in and outside India. Do you have any suggestions to share with readers as to how one can capitalize on such visits?

MS: Sixty per cent of people who visit the networking forums come only when they have a purpose relevant to the event. They mainly visit to build relationships with other people. Following are some suggestions that could be of use:

a. Be excited to participate.
b. Learn about the culture of the place you are visiting. Embrace and enjoy the culture.
c. Believe in first impressions, every action is a chance to impress.
d. Dress up to the event as the locals would do if it will help.
e. Communicate with confidence.

Networking is a business opportunity and it's all about how your attitude is helping the other, and create an impression that makes the other person remember or contact you in the future. Getting a contract through the contact is the objective in most of the networking meetings.

Author: Could you answer the following questions in few words?

Author: Personal branding to you is ...?
MS: Reputation.
Author: What dressing is all about?
MS: Creating an impression when you meet someone.
Author: Power dressing includes?
MS: Appropriate colour combinations in dressing to an event, how you participate in the event, how you smile, how you greet, how you shake hands, how you take and

give your business card, how you stand, how you sit and so on. Everything matters in power dressing.

Author: First thing I observe when I meet a stranger?

MS: Shoes. The shoes tell a lot about a person and cannot be ignored.

Author: Would you like to share your views on personal branding?

MS: Personal branding is important for everyone. You are not just talking to a body sitting or standing in front of you, rather realize that it is to a mind. Every mind has its own emotions, ideas, ideologies, thoughts like ours. If we want to convey something to someone and help them become better, we need to know how the mind functions and be able to break the mind barrier to connect with the other. The quickest way to work on the mind is through the body. A body that is dressed up powerfully can handle any mind and I believe that's one of the strong areas this book also advocates.

*

SHANKAR SRINIVASAN

Shankar Srinivasan has been working in the corporate world for over twenty-five years. He began his career in sales and then hospitality until he joined the Indian Army. After leaving the army, Shankar joined the tourism industry and then the automobile industry where he has spent the last two decades. Working with a range of cultures from Indian to European and Japanese, the journey has shaped his thinking on many fronts.

Do people form an impression about each other when they meet for the first time?

From the moment our eyes catch something or someone, it starts observing and assessing knowingly or unknowingly. The way you dress, present yourself and communicate, all play a major role in imparting your impression on others. It is an involuntary action.

Have you ever experienced any incident where you formed a judgment about a person in a first meeting and then you were proved wrong?

Yes, it's common because the parameters to judge people change with the change in people. We can't fix the parameters to judge the person, and if we judge the person on those fixed parameters then we might judge him/her wrongly.

No one can ever make a hundred per cent exact judgement about a person but we can judge the maximum personality of a person. It might be wrongly or rightly judged.

Do you give people a second chance to change their impression on you?

I do give them a second chance. I actually form a judgement about a person in a first meeting but always leave space to level that judgement in every meeting before making a firm opinion about an individual.

What are the visible factors you look for while forming an impression about others?

Important aspects include:

- Personality
- Confidence
- How you carry yourself
- Your accessories
  You should complement the dress, not the other way around. People should take care of some key things:
- You should be able to adjust yourself according to your surroundings.
- You should never be underdressed or overdressed.
- People know that they have to do something about their dressing sense but they don't know what to do. They

take guidance from books and take advice from people surrounding them. It's basically luck. If you have got the right guidance you grow, otherwise fall.

Can you shed some light on the inspiration that you receive from different cultures?

Actually, I follow six different cultures:

1. Hollywood
2. British
3. German
4. Japanese
5. Army
6. ME

Rather than getting influenced by people, you should do what you want.

Suppose we go to a store, there we see mannequins dressed beautifully. It was done to attract people. But it's not compulsory that the dress that looks good on a mannequin would also suit your personality. Without trying and seeing ourselves in the mirror we cannot purchase that dress.

The same goes for cultures. The top five cultures which I listed are like mannequins and the last one but the most important 'ME' is like trying the mannequins' dresses and selecting the best one for me.

Remember, while choosing your clothes, take care of:

• If you are comfortable or not.
• You should dress according to your age.
• Maintaining basic discipline.

Does the selection of high-level post depend on dressing style of the person or does only competence play a key role?
If you are approached for such a post, then you must have been under observation for some time. The dress you wear on the main interview day is just the reflection of the success you received in your past experiences. So, it's crucial to dress very well on that day just to maintain standards of the position you have been approached for. Also, dressing style must be maintained properly and must be consistent.

Do you think dressing style is an important aspect while climbing the success ladder or is confidence enough?
Confidence is a natural thing which comes through knowledge, experience and understanding. It is a combination of many unseen things that are actually facts. It is a relative term. One might be confident in one context, while in another context he might not. So, we must decide a person's confidence level according to our context need.

Do you think there is a discrimination in Indian companies on dressing on the basis of gender?
The focus of the people is not how one is dressed but how they work.

What would be your advice to the people who want to move up the ladder?
When you move up the ladder, many people have eyes on you and they start assessing your capabilities. People make

a big mistake here of unknowingly jumping up to the next level without confirming whether he/she is ready for the next level or not.

Recognize the expectation of the people and use the opportunities to train yourself.

*

SHINY SURENDRAN

Shiny Surendran is a sports nutritionist with eighteen years of experience. She conducts workshops, speaks at conferences, works in areas of preventive nutrition, metabolic disorders and competitive sports.

What are the things you look at to be healthier from a nutritionist's point of view?

You need to have:

- Energy throughout the day to do the work you want to do.
- Your activeness should be reflected by your skin, hair, eyes.
- To look younger, be active and energetic, people should try to:
  - Have adequate sleep.
  - Eat nourishing food.
  - Focus on the quality of the food they consume.

Do first impressions of people matter to you? Or do you think it is a Western concept?

Yes, it matters a lot to me. It is a natural human tendency to observe others, and how they are dressed, which is what gives us the first impression about others.

I think the first impression is a human concept. Because every individual has an eye on others and they look at how others walk, talk, behave, and dress. So, presenting oneself properly is really important for creating a good impression on others.

Can you share any real-life experience where you formed an impression about someone?
I travel to different places and every day, I interact with lots of new people. So, I create an image for everyone in my mind.

If I have to talk about a particular incident, I would like to share a story about a forty-five-year-old dietician. She is very knowledgeable, no doubt about that. But the way she dresses is a little awkward. For example, if she wears a yellow saree then all her accessories are also yellow, to the extent that even her sandals match her outfit. When I saw her for the very first time, I felt awkward and thought that I should say something to her about how that style doesn't suit her, but then I thought it wouldn't be polite to advise a senior on her dressing style.

In the professional world, one should be really sensitive about how they dress and present themselves to the world.

Is there any difference in the way of presentation of Indian dieticians and your peers from other countries?
Most Indian dieticians wear sarees to conferences and meetings with professionals. It looks good as the Indian female form carries a saree very beautifully. They impress the crowd and leave a mark.

Is there a norm, whether to wear Indian or Western style or should you dress in what you feel is right?

It is one's personal choice. The dressing style of a person is inspired by their environment like home, friends and people surrounding them. No matter what I wear, it should suit my body and most importantly, must be comfortable.

What is your preferred style?

I prefer the saree because it makes one look mature. I prefer sarees for meetings and conferences. But if I have to dress for a sports event, I prefer shirt and trousers. For regular wear, it's not fixed, it's customized.

For every occasion, I dress according to the people who are going to be attending that occasion, and I also try to play with colours and patterns when I dress for a special event.

Do you personally form an impression about people who walk in for consultations?

I have met many knowledgeable people who are not properly groomed. So, I really don't judge people by what they are wearing. The way of one's communication leaves a great impression on me as it shows their thinking style.

If someone walks in for an interview, I will surely look up to see how he/she is dressed, but this doesn't apply to all my clients.

What is your recommendation to upcoming dieticians?

Firstly, they should prefer sarees for official meetings and conferences. They should wear what suits their body type and sober colours should be kept in mind. They should wear minimal accessories as their image in people's mind is that of a doctor. So, they should maintain a personality which reflects their profession.

*

TEN

STYLE ICONS OF TOMORROW

STYLES ICONS OF TOMORROW are experts in their respective fields. They are people who are always dressed to make an impact or statement. They are role models for power dressing, style and charisma for youngsters and upcoming professionals.

VIKRAM COTAH

Vikram Cotah is a hotelier by profession and a foodie at heart. He is the Chief Operating Officer of GRT Hotels and Resorts, the fastest growing chain of hotels in south India. He is also a health advocate and a fitness enthusiast.

Q. Do you think we form impressions when we meet people?
A. Definitely, yes. I strongly believe that the first impression
is a lasting impression and you have to win that moment to
build a successful relationship. It is human nature to like
good-looking people and good-looking people always means
well-groomed people.

Q. What are some aspects that contribute to forming
first impressions?
A. The main aspects of forming first impressions are the
attitude of the person, the personality of the person, how
the person dresses for the occasion and, most importantly,
how he exudes enthusiasm and interest in the other person.
Needless to say, hygiene and grooming play an important role
in making the first impact.

Q. How does this impact your further interaction with
the person?
A. The first impression always sets the tone for the relationship.
Once you score a win on this, your interaction with the
other person will be easier to manage and you can have an
advantage of creating a long-term impression. Basically, the
other person starts liking you and we do extra special things
if we like someone.

Q. What is the first thing that you observe in a person when
you meet them?
A. I personally notice the body language and the confidence,
the smile, the grooming, dress sense and attitude.

Q. Is personal branding important in your profession?

A. Yes, it plays an important role for success. This is not only in my profession but in most of the professions which deal with people.

Q. What is your personal brand?

A. My personal brand that I project is of a professional hotelier and a restauranter.

Q. Do you consciously work on your branding? If yes, how?

A. I work on my brand in the following ways:

- I THINK of myself as a brand.
- I project my brand in social media very purposefully.
- I make sure I am seen at relevant events and participate as keynote speaker in events which project me as a successful hotelier.

I have a personal blog, www.guestsaregods.com, where I share my experiences and I am active on LinkedIn.

I audit my brand regularly and see how I am being projected in different media.

I also work on my wardrobe and dressing to ensure that I project my brand always, be it power dressing for boardrooms or party dressing for casual events.

Q. Who has impacted you the most when it comes to branding and dressing?

A. My heroes have been Anand Mahindra, JRD Tata, Shah Rukh Khan and Narendra Modi.

Q. Complete the sentences:
- As a brand, I stand for – passion for hospitality.
- First impressions are – always lasting impressions.
- Dressing appropriately is – the first step in branding.

*

DR INDU BALLANI

Dr Indu Ballani (MD Dermatology) is a practising cosmetic dermatologist with twelve years of experience based in New Delhi. She is also a visiting consultant at BL Kapoor Hospital, New Delhi. She runs a centre which provides lasers and cosmetic procedures including injectables and treatment for anti-aging and skin rejuvenation. Indu also trains young dermatologists in injectable procedures.

Q. Tell us something about yourself.
A. I am an aesthetic dermatologist. True to the nature of a doctor, I am always looking for ways to help my clients and make a difference in their lives as so many of them approach me hoping for a welcome change and place a lot of trust in my hands. I am a mother of two and have really enjoyed raising my kids. I hardly lose my temper and stay extremely calm. I do believe my calmness is the most dominant part of my personality.

Q. Do you think we form impressions of people when we meet them?

A. Yes, we do form impressions of people based on the way they carry themselves. In a well exposed world like ours, we tend to bank upon our own perspectives of people and are quick to judge.

Q. What are some of the aspects that contribute to forming first impressions?

A. The way people dress, their personality and etiquette.

Q. How does this impact your further interaction with the person?

A. It does not impact my interaction because it is my job to make all my clients very comfortable. My sessions with clients usually involve very sensitive treatments, hence my temperament remains the same for all – comforting and caring.

Q. What is the first thing that you observe in a person when you meet them?

A. Even before words are spoken, it is the clothing and body language that comes to my notice.

Q. Is personal branding important in your profession?

A. Personal branding today is important in any and every profession. Yes, it is the most important in my profession. Just the way I would form a judgement about a person when I meet him/her, people judge me the same way and form impressions. The kind of audience I interact with and work on is a very evolved audience. So, before they buy my service, they absolutely buy the brand that I am and how I walk the talk.

It is about establishing a connect with the clients and that's only possible if they relate with me and my brand personality.

Q. What is your personal brand?
A. I have a personal stylist who takes care of my wardrobe choices, so while I am busy helping other people with their skin, someone makes sure I look my best while I do it. I am pro social media. I believe a strong connect can be built on the platform with the audience I wish to connect with.

Q. Do you consciously work on your branding? If yes, how?
Yes, I do. I keep up with trends and constantly educate myself with industry knowledge. People place a lot of trust in me and I have to make sure I am offering the best expert advice at every session.

Q. Who has impacted you the most when it comes to branding and dressing?
A. The millennials have played a major role in inspiring me to constantly make efforts in brand building. My personal stylist has changed the way I conduct myself. I find myself at international conferences and important events looking the part and that has changed the way people perceive me.

Q. Complete the sentences:
- As a brand, I stand for – perseverance, sincerity and clarity.
- First impressions are – lasting ones, they make or break deals.
- Dressing appropriately is – of utmost importance as it demonstrates one's respect towards occasions and people.

*

DR PREETHI PRADHAN

Dr Preethi Pradhan is a healthcare management professional with twenty years of experience. She completed her Masters from Tata Institute of Social Sciences, Mumbai and holds a PhD in Health Policy and Management from IIT Madras. She is currently the Dean at Chitkara School of Health Sciences, Chitkara University, Chandigarh. She has worked for over a decade at the WHO Collaborating Centre of Aravind Eye Care System.

Preeti has experience and expertise of teaching, training, mentoring and coaching health management and leadership professionals and has been actively involved in design and implementation of various courses. She was recently listed in the top fifty global women healthcare leaders.

Q. Tell us something about yourself.
A. I am a professor. I am enthusiastic about life and love my work. It feels great to be part of a group which is a catalyst in changing an adolescent to a young adult with a purpose. I love being with people and leading large teams.

Q. Do you think we form impressions of people when we meet them?
A. We definitely do. It takes a lot of self-control and self-discipline to suspend judgements and biases. Some people

may delay forming an impression till they spend more time with that person and get to understand him/her.

Q. What are some aspects that contribute to forming first impressions?

A. One's own upbringing, culture, religion, experiences and context. We can draw different first impressions depending on what we see the person doing first-hand, such as volunteering at a temple versus driving very fast versus dancing at a party versus sitting quietly in a park.

Q. How does this impact your further interaction with the person?

A. We will bring our impression in a future interaction in a different context. We may label the person or expect them to conform to our lopsided conclusion about the potential behaviour of the person.

Q. Is personal branding important in your profession?

A. Yes. Professions have their own branding. So, yes, definitely, when so many eyes see you on a daily basis.

Q. What is your personal brand?

A. Simplicity, good self-confidence, friendly.

Q. Complete the sentences:

- As a brand, I stand for – energy, confidence and quiet strength.
- First impressions are – just first impressions but may not be the true picture of a person.

- Dressing appropriately is – very important as it shows respect to the other.

*

DR RICHA KATIYAR

Dr Richa Katiyar is among the leading fertility and IVF specialists in India and is the Managing Director at Hope Fertility in New Delhi. She has a Fellowship in Reproductive Medicine from Germany and did her MD from the prestigious All India Institute of Medical Sciences (AIIMS).

Richa has received many international and national awards, including Global Indian of the Year Award, given to her by our past President, Honorable Smt. Pratibha Devi Singh Patil, for her contribution to the field of infertility.

Q. Do you think we form impressions of people when we meet them?
A. Yes, first impressions might not be the last impression, but they are definitely not fleeting.

Q. What are some of the aspects that contribute to forming first impressions?
A. Eye contact, confidence, expressions and handshake.

Q. How does this impact your further interaction with the person?

A. The first impression decides whether I would want to get warm and friendly with the person or remain distant and take my time to understand them better.

Q. What is the first thing that you observe in a person when you meet them?

A. Their neatness, which reflects on their personality.

Q. Is personal branding important in your profession?

A. Yes.

Q. Do you consciously work on your branding?

A. Yes. In this age of Internet, the best way to promote the brand is by using social media sites like Instagram, Pinterest, Tumblr, Facebook and Google Reviews.

Q. Complete the sentences:

- As a brand, I stand for – originality and simplicity.
- First impressions are – lasting impressions.
- Dressing appropriately is – a sign of who you are.

*

AMITAVA SINHA

Amitava Sinha has more than twenty years of experience in the automotive industry. He began his career with Indian auto giant Tata Motors in 1994 as Sr. Engineer – Process Quality, then experienced fast-track growth with General Motors for nine years as General Manager. He worked with AVTEC Ltd for two years as Vice President to manage overall Purchase and Supply chain function, and with Daimler India Commercial Vehicles.

In 2012, Amitava joined Linamar India Pvt Ltd to set up a greenfield facility. He is also a Board Member for Linamar India Pvt Ltd and Jaya Hind Montupet Joint Venture.

Q. Do you think we form impressions of people when we meet them?

A. Yes, for sure. Some may be long lasting and some may be temporary.

Q. What are some of the aspects that contribute to forming first impressions?

A. Your appearance, how you conduct yourself, selection of words, dressing, body language and comfort level of individuals given a situation. Overall, how you carry yourself forms the first impression.

Q. How does this impact your further interaction with the person?

A. First impressions to some extent decide how approachable a person is. Whether you feel comfortable about approaching this person further. You decide if further interaction is going to add value to you and to your organization. As the popular saying goes, first impression is the last impression. Though not a hundred per cent true, but to some extent it is.

Q. What is the first thing that you observe in a person when you meet them?

A. Overall personality but truly how one looks or the appearance of the person.

Q. Is personal branding important in your profession?

A. Yes, individuality and therefore personal branding is important in all professions be it corporate, sports or entertainment.

Q. What is your personal brand?

A. Personal branding is what I stand for irrespective of the situation. Upfront and straightforward and no compromise on integrity.

Q. Do you consciously work on your branding?

A. No. As it is a part of me now and has become natural. However, I do remind myself from time to time.

Q. Who has impacted you the most when it comes to branding and dressing?

A. If I have to name an individual, it will be Mr Sudhir Rao, Ex-CEO of Skoda India.

Q. Complete the sentences:

• As a brand, I stand for – integrity.

- First impressions are – as important as your other skills, attributes and competence.
- Dressing appropriately is – dressing right for work and play.

*

RAKHI KISHORE

Rakhi Kishore is a radio jockey, TV host, theatre actor and communication specialist.

Q. Tell us something about yourself.
A. I'm a bold and confident person who is difficult to intimidate. A thorough professional, I respect and love my work. I also strongly believe that we all must give back to the society in our own unique ways and hence, I am constantly involved in various activities that involve children, the elderly and animals.

Q. Do you think we form impressions of people when we meet them?
A. Definitely!

Q. What are some of the aspects that contribute to forming first impressions?
A. Our looks, dressing sense, mannerism, body language, our voice and speech, and also our aura that reflects our inner self.

Q. How does this impact your further interaction with the person?

A. It certainly decides the extent, depth and the duration of the interaction.

Q. What is the first thing that you observe in a person when you meet them?

A. The first thing I observe is their look, body posture and facial expressions.

Q. Is personal branding important in your profession?

A. It is.

Q. What is your personal brand?

A. Confident, honest, bold, comfortable and bright – whether it's the dress, the demeanour, the expressions or the speech. Positivity and honesty is my brand.

Q. Do you consciously work on your branding?

A. Not exactly. I feel that over a period of time our professional and personal experiences, plus our observations and updates on society, and people around us evolves us as humans and influences our persona to a great extent. One will always emerge as the person his thoughts and beliefs are made up of.

Q. Who has impacted you the most when it comes to branding and dressing?

A. No one in particular.

Q. Complete the sentences:

• As a brand, I stand for – confidence.

- First impressions are – substantial but not everlasting.
- Dressing appropriately is – an integral part of living.

*

DR SUDHAKAR PANJU

Dr Sudhakar Panju is a dental implantologist with a professional practice of seventeen years since 1999. He runs an academy, B.I.T.E, where they have trained more than 400 dentists on advanced procedures. He is also the Regional Training Director for a business organization.

Q. Do you think we form impressions of people when we meet them?
A. Yes. Our brain keeps doing it subconsciously.

Q. What are some of the aspects that contribute to forming first impressions?
A. Greetings, looks, communication, style of dressing, accessories and gestures.

Q. How does this impact your further interaction with the person?
A. There is an inner intuition that says whether to proceed or to move away.

Q. What is the first thing that you observe in a person when you meet them?
A. Bright face and it should carry a smile.

Q. Is personal branding important in your profession?
A. I am the brand in my profession. People come only for me.

Q. What is your personal brand?
A. Communication, sense of humour, neatness, creativity, dependability, trustworthy and fun to be with.

Q. Do you consciously work on your branding?
A. I think, yes. I know my strength.

Q. Who has impacted you the most when it comes to branding and dressing?
A. Kamal Haasan.

Q. Complete the sentences:
- As a brand, I stand for – trustworthiness.
- First impressions are – long standing.
- Dressing appropriately is – one of the best ways to win people's hearts.

ELEVEN

TEN COMMANDMENTS

AS A QUICK REMINDER of the above chapters, the following ten commandments in each category can help you power dress efficiently.

DRESSING

- Your choice of clothes speaks volumes about your personality and the image you want to portray.
- Dressing well is important as it creates an impression of you to others.
- Whether you are a man or a woman, power dress to highlight your position of importance in society.

- While dressing and external appearance are important, it is also essential that you work on your 'internal wiring'.
- Use the four levels of dressing wisely amd according to occasion. Remember, it is not necessary to wear a matte suit for every meeting.
- Pick your clothes depending on your body shape as this gives you a better silhouette.
- Always look professional. Do not just dress yourself; think about whom and what you are dressing for.
- Your attention to detail at dressing speaks volumes about your attention to details elsewhere.
- Imitation of others' dress sense is never a good rule to follow as it makes you look uncomfortable.
- Combine power dressing with the other rules of image management to create a powerful brand called you.

STYLING

- Style should be synonymous with comfort. If you aren't comfortable or cannot carry off a particular style, it becomes more of a burden than a style quotient.
- Always dress to represent your company, your position and yourself. However, make sure you adhere to the dressing norms of the country you are in.
- Project visually what you want others to see through your attire, grooming and body language.

- It is always better to be a first you, rather than a second someone! Just dress the way that suits you and your style!
- If something does not match your own style, culture or value systems you should not wear it.
- Styling is not limited to dressing. Styling comes into other aspects as well, such as doing your hair, make-up and personal grooming.
- Elegance and simplicity are everlasting companions of style.
- Try not to overindulge and wear too many styles at once.
- Remember that style statements at work should not coincide with casual fashion.
- Create your own style and own it.

GROOMING

- As an important element of image, grooming is as essential as dressing, attire and etiquette.
- Hygiene is an essential part of grooming. Presenting yourself in a neat and clean way helps enhance your image.
- Grooming takes into account self-maintenance as part of basic hygiene.
- Grooming essentially takes into account hair, skin and clothes.
- Proper grooming takes the unnecessary spotlight away from you allowing people to focus on the essentials of what you are saying.
- Personal grooming done right tells people what you think about yourself.

- Always pay attention to avoid image breakers.
- Women should keep an eye on make-up, hair, nails and fragrance while grooming.
- Men must take measures to groom their beard and moustache, have a proper haircut and most importantly avoid body odour.
- Grooming done right exhibits an individual's natural beauty.

ETIQUETTE

- Etiquette is a complex term that combines good manners, social skills and appropriate behaviour in various situations.
- Although image management deals with business etiquette, the basis of it begins from a much earlier age.
- Several principles of family and social etiquette are transferable onto professional and business etiquette.
- In terms of image, etiquette is part of your body language and behaviour.
- It is complementary to dressing and other aspects of image when it comes to creating a great first impression.
- Etiquette speaks volumes about your personality, background, education and culture.
- Corporate etiquette is essential in image management, especially during interactions with people from different cultures and countries.
- Good etiquette can help break communication barriers in different social situations.

- The importance of etiquette is such that a lack of it can stop you from being a global citizen and achieving opportunities that may otherwise put you on an international platform.
- The good news is that you can always learn and improve your etiquette skills.

ACKNOWLEDGEMENTS

IT WAS SOMETIME DURING 2014 that my friend Vijay insisted a few times that I should write a book on image management, and I always laughed it off. The seed of the idea planted then germinated about two years later during a workshop in Chennai when I seriously started pondering over it. I realized that many people around me were struggling in their professions and business not because of lack of skill or will, but due to lack of self-confidence. I decided to write a book so that I could share my knowledge through some easy and doable steps which would help people present themselves confidently in a professional situation. The whole idea was to help an Indian become a global Indian – proud of Indian ethos with the confidence and aspirations of a global citizen.

I discussed the idea with Murali Sundaram, my writing coach, who was immediately hooked on to it and insisted that

I commit a start date to the book. He did a lot of hand holding during the initial phase by concretizing the ideas, structuring my thought process and guiding me on the fundamentals of book writing. Thank you Murali for helping me kick-start this book.

Throughout the writing process and even while finalizing the name of the book itself, I found that *Dressology* is about striking a right balance between two seemingly diverse concepts of logic and creativity – concepts that I imbibed from my father and mother, respectively. My mother was the first image consultant of my life. She just knew how to create the right impression for every occasion. My father, an engineer, was more logical and was more into methods and systems. Therefore, the book is an attempt to explain the science behind the art of dressing.

A heartfelt gratitude also goes to my teachers and the principal of my school who were my role models in grace and poise. The way they carried themselves and taught us to mind our P's and Q's ensured we were groomed 'right'. All this subconscious childhood learning manifested into awareness and knowledge when the science behind it was taught by my teachers at the image consulting institute.

My profession as a trainer, coach and educator enabled me to interact with people from different parts of India and abroad, and they have contributed to a fair share of my learning. I want to thank my students and clients who made me learn, improvise and adapt new concept and methods. I also thank all the esteemed people who took time out of their busy schedules and willingly shared their experiences and knowledge during the interviews.

I am extremely grateful to my guiding stars who ensured that I didn't lose sight of my goals and have always pushed me hard to bring out the best in me. I can't thank you enough – Surendran Jeysekar, Biju Chandran, Karan Hasija, Rajiv Taleja and Shweta Vij. Your motivation and support make me what I am and what I will be.

I don't have words to express my love for my three biggest critiques and admirers – my husband, Bhupesh, and my daughters, Himanshi and Priyanshi. Their contribution in my life is immeasurable and invaluable.

The book would not have got its present form without the support of Bharath and his team (for editing), Vishal Mardia (for the illustrations), my publishers, Rajdeep Mukherjee and Sushmita Chatterjee (Pan Macmillan India). Thank you so much for turning my convictions into a book.